THE

WHIFFLE

BALL

KILLER

THE SECOND EDITION

By

Karen Roberts

K.K. Roberts
Book

KK Roberts Books US
PO Box 363
Ridgefield, WA 98642
Visit my website: kkrobertsbooks.us

Paperback
ISBN: 979-8-9886431-2-8
eISBN: 979-8-9886431-3-5

TABLE OF CONTENTS

BRING ON THE LIGHT

I'm sitting in a church meeting. Abby, a middle-aged woman with gray, short, straight hair, comes up to me. "Karen," Abby says, "I found a passage in the Bible that is about you." She opens her Bible to the "The Gospel According to John" and reads, "… the light has come into the world, and men loved darkness rather than light, because their deeds were evil. For every one who does evil hates the light, and does not come to the light, lest his deeds should be exposed." RSV 3.19–20.

I have a questioning expression. Is this woman saying I love evil? "I don't love darkness," I respond, shaking my head.

She explains, "You will expose the darkness with light." She smiles warmly.

"I'm not so sure about that," I say. "I'm usually one step behind the darkness; even when I need to be one step ahead."

"But you know where the darkness is," Abby says. "And this"—she shows me another passage about light in "The First Letter of John" and reads—"'If we say we have fellowship with him while we walk in darkness, we lie and do not live according to the truth. RSV 1.6' Does that remind you of anyone?"

I shake my head. "I moved on. I'm done with him." I don't want to go down that road again.

"Yes, but he's not done with you," Abby says. This is uncomfortable, so I walk away.

Over the many years, there have been many people without a name. I don't know who they are. I'll assign names mostly in alphabetical order, in order of appearance. Abby isn't her real name. It is just the first name starting with the letter A.

There is no rain, but the sky is cloudy and the ground is moist from last night's rain. The leaves have turned from green to orange. The branches have turned crisp. In the neighbor's yard, his garden rake has left stripes of leaves across the lawn. I'm walking out to my car. I parked in front of the church. A woman I don't know follows after me calling, "Mary, Mary." I'll call her Ada. She is short and thin with black witchy shoulder- length hair poking out in all directions. She has a long face, like a donkey. She is leaning forward with her hand out as if she is hailing a taxi and stepping out into the parking lot in front of the church. There is a tall, athletic man with light-brown hair walking after her, but lagging on the steps just outside the entrance door. He has light skin, a round face, and blue eyes. I'll call him Adam. I look around. There are no other women in the front parking lot and I realize Ada is calling to me.

This is exasperating, I try to make light of her mistake, and say, "This reminds me of the time I worked in Seattle and there were two Karens and two Marys who worked there. A new employee started calling me Mary."

"So, you decided to change your name to Mary?" Ada asks. She is trying to be helpful and acting like she is talking to someone who is mentally deficient. Adam is behind her trying to silence her. Ada says to Adam, "Wait, I'm onto something," and looks back at me hopefully.

"No, you're not," Adam says like he's talking to an idiot. "All she knows is that you're following after her and calling her the wrong name." Ada looks down to the side, frowns, and walks away with Adam. A normal conversation would have included an apology. They leave. I drive home and brush it off.

Later I'm at the store. Two women come up to me, Alana and Alayna. Alana asks, "Mother of the messiah, right?" Alana is hoping she was talking with the right person. I look around. Everyone else is going about their day, pushing a grocery cart and intently heading straight to the next item on a list. I wish I was them.

Alayna asks me, "Do you believe a woman can get pregnant without having sex?"

I'm assuming this is a theological question, so I quote, "With God all things are possible." This was a mistake.

"Do you believe you might be pregnant?" Alana asks.

"I don't know," I respond. I didn't have a reason to think about it. I'm hoping Alana and Alayna will go away. Unfortunately, this was just the beginning.

I'm approached by an angry man in the church lobby. He is short with medium-dark brown hair. He doesn't attend our church. His face is wide and flushed. He has sweat on his forehead and pursed lips. Allen accuses, "What are you? Some sort of pervert?"

"Excuse me?" I ask with forced calm.

"It says right here in the Bible, 'so shall thy sons espouse thee,'" Allen reads. He taps his finger on the page. "This passage is about you. Do you have sex with your sons?"

"Where is this passage?" I ask. "I'd like to read it in context." I read The Book of Isaiah Chapter 62.

A church member asks, "How do you give birth to a son if you need your son to espouse you?"

I nod in agreement with the church member. "I was thinking the same thing." Allen rolls his eyes. The pastor and a few elders from the church lead him away.

Another one, Amy, shows up at the church to ask questions that will give transparency to my funding. I explain to Amy, "I don't have funding. I donate to the church."

Another, Annette, shows up at my work and admits, "We are given a script to follow. We aren't told what to do if the script doesn't work." She had snuck past security. A group of six pickers quickly assemble to escort her to the main entrance.

This happened repeatedly at the church, at the grocery store, at work, at the graduate college. I called the local police department and they were disturbed by the amount, but little was done. If I called the police in the area of my work, my next action would be packing up my things and turning in my building keys or security badge to never return. Or my items would be mailed to me. At my graduate college, I was expelled for religious discrimination, because I didn't refute a student's "mother of the messiah" comment strong enough. One class left to complete my degree, a 3.67 GPA, and my thesis finished and defended. I'm in the middle of fighting the expulsion now and requesting an explanation.

I changed to attend a synagogue and it happened there too. I called to find out who has jurisdiction in the area of the synagogue. I was told it was the sheriff's office. So, I called the sheriff's office for their assistance. The sheriff was intuitive and responsive to the problem.

"They must be social workers," the sheriff considers. "They must think you were found incompetent."

"I wasn't found incompetent," I corrected.

"Yes, that is what I figured," the sheriff says. "Otherwise, you wouldn't be confused as to why they are doing this. It must be from a family member. Who would do something like this?" the sheriff asks.

"I had a protection order against my ex-husband. Although it is expired now," I inform him.

"What year?" the sheriff asks.

"1986," I say.

"Too long ago, he wouldn't have a reason to do this now," the sheriff decides. "It must be someone else."

"Once the Yakima Police Department told me my mother called them," I remember. "But later they admitted that 'mother' was just a generic word to refer to any family member. Later the Yakima Police told me it was my father."

"It was probably neither," the sheriff decides.

"I don't know," I say. I was about to add that the FBI told me once that my ex-husband was calling people and pretending to be my father, but we already eliminated my first ex-husband and I know it wasn't my second ex-husband.

"Well, what they are doing is illegal," the sheriff assures. "If they do this again in our jurisdiction, just call us and we'll come right away." Unfortunately, I'm not usually in his jurisdiction. I wish I was.

The rabbi schedules a meeting with me for Monday at 7:00 p.m. I need to rearrange my workday to ensure I'm there on time. I stop to buy burgers and fries because I don't have time to eat dinner. The burger tastes old and the fries are stale. I eat it in the car on the way to the synagogue. I arrive at the synagogue on time, hoping the rabbi will be pleased that I am prompt. To my complete disappointment, the rabbi informs me I'm no longer allowed to participate or attend, because I involved the police. I'm to leave, return any books I've borrowed, and never come back. This was the reason for the meeting. The rabbi could have just done this over the phone. Every effort I make to address this problem just puts me further behind.

Just this week two more social workers snuck past Security at my work. I'll go into that later. First, there is a story I've never told.

1983

I meet Daniel Bondehagen at a college-age group at the Auburn Free Methodist Church. He has balding blond hair, a bristly blond mustache, and blue eyes. He is 5'11" tall and slender. He is sitting and listening intently to the pastor. But he notices the Seattle Pacific University emblem on my sweater. "Do you go to Seattle Pacific University?" he asks.

"No, I go to Green River Community College," I reply. "My sister went to Seattle Pacific University."

"My friends tell me I look like Tom Petty," Daniel confesses. "Do I look like Tom Petty?" he asks.

"I don't know who Tom Petty is," I respond. Daniel decides that is the best answer.

Daniel hopes to become a youth pastor and then possibly a lead pastor. He is earning a Theology degree at Seattle Pacific University. Both of his parents have bachelor's degrees in theology. Visions of becoming a pastor's wife start to spark. Other members of the group say, "They're not pastors."

Daniel is living with his parents, Thomas and Viola Bondehagen. Daniel invites me to his parent's home to see him and have Sunday dinner with his parents after church. They live in a simple three-bedroom house. The house is painted seafoam green with white trim. The interior walls are pale seafoam green. The carpet is seafoam green with soft pastel flowers. The sofa is dark seafoam green with a soft raised pattern. The swivel rocker is upholstered in seafoam green linen. I ask about the color scheme.

Viola says, "Seafoam green creates a feeling of calm," and smiles wide. Her teeth glisten in the sunlight. "We want our guests to feel calm." Viola is a homemaker, a short woman with a short body and long legs, gray hair, hazel eyes, and large buck teeth. Thomas is a retired, postal worker and war veteran. He is a short man with a long body and short legs, gray-blue eyes, gray hair, and is 100% Norwegian. Together they produced three tall children. Thomas is lying on the floor because it is better for his back than sleeping on the mattress.

I am living in a two-bedroom apartment off M Street in Auburn with roommates, Liz and Carla. Liz is short but cute with blue eyes and blonde hair. Carla is taller with black hair, a round face, and a wide smile. Liz and Carla share the largest bedroom. I sub-rent the smaller room for $90/month. My monthly budget is small. Cleaning pays $3/hour.

I'm a "starving college student." This was a full meal, my only full meal all week. I praise Viola, "Thank you. That was lovely." It was an ordinary meat and potato dinner, but the hospitality was nice.

Daniel thought I should have thanked Thomas too. "He provided the money for the food," he chastised.

In another week, Daniel decides I should meet his siblings. I meet Daniel's brothers and sister. His oldest brother, David, is ten years older. His second oldest brother, John, is nine years older. They seem like nice people. David explains, "After we moved out, they had the seafoam green explosion." Viola shushes David. They say the Free Methodists should be called shackled Methodists because they don't allow drinking or dancing.

I say, "That doesn't make sense. Think of the song, 'The Lord of the Dance.'"

Viola gasps, "It's a song about Satan."

"No, it isn't," and I sing, "I danced for the scribes and the Pharisees, but they would not dance and they wouldn't follow me. I danced for the fisherman for James and for John. They came with me and the dance went on." I sing enough for them to understand the song is about Jesus.

"Sing it for Daniel," says John. David nods. But I stay quiet and look up at Viola.

The whole time I sang, Viola was yelling at me to stop. Dan wonders why I didn't listen to his mother and stop singing. I justify my actions by explaining, "They needed to understand what the song is about." They need to understand I would sing about Jesus, not Satan. I refuse to apologize.

We sit on the floor and play a board game together in the living room called "Scotland Yard." The game is a replica of the public transit system in London. The object of the game is to intercept the villain, Mr. X, using different routes.

Viola came out of the kitchen and told of the time she was addicted to phenobarbital: "The good Lord healed me of it. I went to a prayer meeting. The man put his hand on me and said, 'this woman has trouble with forgiveness.' I didn't know I had trouble with forgiveness, but I did. I was slain in the Spirit and fell straight to the ground."

I asked, "Did this happen before or after you became a preacher?" Viola stops and looks at me stunned.

John says, "She was just filling in with preaching. She was never a pastor. That is an exaggeration."

Her daughter, Ruth, brags, "I'm so proud of her. She has done so many things. She has been a preacher, a clerk, a piano teacher, and an Avon Lady." Viola looks at me and then starts to cry.

Ruth complains to me, "She is crying in the kitchen because of what you said." All I brought up was that Viola said she was a preacher.

John quietly said to his sister, "It is because of your 'Avon Lady' comment." Ruth gives him a surprised and uncomprehending look. "This is becoming a pyramid scheme like Amway." Ruth remains confused and looks down at the seafoam green carpet.

We eat dinner and their sons and daughter leave. I'm getting ready to leave as well. Thomas is sitting on the couch watching TV. Viola is standing behind him, leaning forward against the couch. Thomas says to me, "You should work as an 'Avon Lady.' It shows you can bring home some money for the family." Viola has a proud look on her face.

I heard about Amway from a high school friend. If this pyramid scheme was anything like it, I was out. "I wouldn't qualify," I respond. "I don't even wear makeup."

Viola responds, "What does that have to do with anything." I turn back toward the dining room to find my purse. I left it in my chair.

Thomas continues to watch TV and says to Viola, "Old Man Withers is good for the money, isn't he? He says he just closes his eyes and pretends you're someone else." He chuckles. Viola's proud facial expression turns sad and vacant.

"I need to get going." I was already heading for the door. They startle as if they forgot I was there.

Later a woman who knows Viola comes by my apartment. I'll call her Alyce. I assume Alyce is from the Free Methodist church. I step outside to talk with her. Alyce asks me about the conversation Viola had in the living room with Thomas. I repeat it back the best that I can remember, including her son's comment about the pyramid scheme.

"Avon isn't a pyramid scheme," informs Alyce.

A tall thin man who lives at the apartment complex is listening to our conversation. I'll call him Andy. "Has she ever tried to sell you Avon?" Andy asks in a twangy voice.

"No," I answer. That is odd. "I never wear makeup. It would be a waste of time," I excuse.

Andy says gruffly, "I want to be on her list of clients."

Alyce interrupts, "Stay away from him. There is something wrong with him." I don't know who to stay away from. I go inside my apartment and shut the door.

Andy yells, "Didn't you hear her? They are trying to get her to…." The conversation trails off.

Alyce responds, "I don't want her to think of Viola that way."

Andy snaps back, "You aren't her friend. You stay away from her."

Carla comes out of her bedroom and pulls back the living room curtains to peek out the window. Carla asks, "What was that about? All I heard was 'You aren't her friend. You stay away from her.'"

13

I answer, "I'm not sure." I open the apartment door and lookout. I don't see either of them. I never see them again.

I relayed the conversation to Daniel. Daniel tells me, "A woman from the church wouldn't have come by your apartment. They have an index card you need to fill out for visitation. The woman must have been from somewhere else." Daniel asks me, "What would you do if I tried to strangle you from behind?"

"I would break your ribs," I immediately respond.

Daniel imagines for a moment and then laughs, "Then I would become like Adam, with one rib missing. Get it? Missing a rib." He laughs again. He is referring to the Adam and Eve story in the Book of Genesis. Daniel tells this to the college group at the church.

Dale is a nice man who never dates. He is a member of the college group and a strong Christian. He is nice-looking, short with dishwater blond hair. I overhear Dale ask the pastor, "Should we warn her about him?"

"No, he seems fine with her," the pastor responds to Dale. They are talking about me. I'm proud someone is fine with me; although, I don't know what the conversation refers to.

Daniel explains the pastor was counseling him on pornography and marijuana use, which were problems in his past. "The best pastors have a darker history and turn it around," Daniel says. "They give the best sermons. Our pastor is a good man. He is the one who turned me on to the idea of becoming a pastor."

"I'm going to stay up at the college and study," I inform him so he knows my plans. "I need to read this textbook, and I'm not that good of a reader."

He tells me of a friend he met at college. "Do you read backward?" Daniel asks. "I have a friend with dyslexia. He reads everything backward." He laughs. "He is going bald like me. He started pulling at his hair and it all started falling out onto the desktop. He looked down at the pile of hair he pulled out and started screaming." He laughs. Then he looks serious and adds, "I've decided never to do that." He frowns. "He can't grow a proper mustache, unlike me, but he keeps trying." Laughs again. "We both decided this is the best haircut for hiding baldness and vowed never to comb it to the side." He looks at me and smiles again.

Dale interjects, "He isn't talking about a college student." He clarifies, "He is talking about someone who visits him at college."

Daniel says, "I haven't seen him for a while: one month, six weeks." He is evasive in his answer. I get the impression they used to smoke marijuana together.

Daniel asks me if he can take me out for dinner. "The pastor told me, 'The secret to a great relationship is to treat even the cheapest restaurant as an expensive night out. That way you can always have an expensive night out together.' He suggested McDonalds." We drive to the McDonalds parking lot in his parent's car, a four-door Buick with a seafoam green exterior. "My parents had to look hard to find a car with an interior that matches the exterior. Isn't that nice?" I nod. Daniel let me know what he wanted and handed me a $10 bill. "Maybe we'll see Patches the Clown," he laughed. He disappears to the back of McDonalds. Completely disappears. I go in to wait in line, assuming he will join me soon.

As I'm in line to order, a man with straight brown hair comes running to the front lobby. The top part of his hair that he brushes over his bald spot is sticking up at an angle. He tells the cashier, "Hey, we had to clear the children out of the playground." He looks over at me with an intense frown. I'm patiently waiting for my turn to order. I put in the order, and I'm given the burgers in two "to go" bags.

I look down at the "to go" bags. "I was hoping for dine-in," I explain to the cashier.

The cashier shakes his head. "No dine-in," he asserts and moves his hand flat in a firm horizontal motion.

I don't see Daniel. I don't see him anywhere. I take the "to go" bags and walk out into the parking lot. I look for his parent's car. Daniel is sitting in the driver's seat. I go in and sit next to him. "Patches was there," he says miserably. I look behind me at the playground and don't see anyone. Most of the playground is out of view from the car. Maybe if I go out to look around the corner…. Daniel quickly grabs one of the "to go" bags out of my hands, takes a large handful of fries, and stuffs them in his mouth. His mouth is in a full circle now and the fries are hanging halfway out.

I wonder if he grabbed the right bag. It was a 50/50 chance, and he got the right bag. I'm relieved my order was in my hands. I didn't want to be stuck eating a cheeseburger with American cheese. "Do you want your change?" I ask, handing back the coins.

He smacks the change out of my hand and onto the floor in front of the driver seat. "Wait, I wanted that." He smiles at me and bends over to pick up the money. It isn't a friendly smile or a pleasing smile, as I expected, but a tense smile. He places the change in the pocket on the driver-side door. I sit next to him and quietly eat my burger. This was his first date with a girl ever and I had expected first date jitters. I tell myself it will get better.

In the parking lot, I hear, "Hey, she just got in the car with him."

The McDonalds manager said, "I figured he was here with someone."

I silently wonder who they are talking about. I look and don't see anyone in the parking lot. I see no one in the parked cars. I see no moving cars. Maybe they are on the other side that is blocked from view. There doesn't appear to be a road there. Maybe I'll come back another day to see what is on the other side of the restaurant.

We finish our meal and then drive to his parents' house. Daniel says something about a man who buried people in the crawl space. Daniel questions, "Do you think it's a good idea?"

"I think it would smell," I answer.

"Smell?" he asks.

I explain, "Even when my parents had mice that died in the wall, the bodies would smell as they decomposed."

"Your parents had bodies in the wall?" he asks.

"Mice," I emphasize. "My parents had mice. The mice nested in the wall and some died. Their bodies decomposed as they died." They cleaned up the mess and reconstructed the wall.

"That would explain why he was caught so early," he pondered. He was talking again about some man on the news. I don't follow the story. "He finally wised up and started burying them and dumping them in the river."

I don't know who Daniel is talking about. When we arrive at his parents' house with the empty McDonalds bags I ask them, "Who is Patches the Clown?"

"We never should have told him that story," Thomas says. "We have to check the McDonalds to make sure there is no picture of Ronald. A statue is worse."

Viola nods. "Go to a restaurant, but avoid McDonalds," she advises.

When I return to my apartment, I call my mother and ask, "Who is Patches the Clown? Was it that man on Channel 12?"

"That was Captain Kangaroo," she corrects. "I don't know who Patches the Clown would be."

Liz overhears my conversation, "Obviously," she says, "Patches is a clown who entertains children. That's all you need to know." I decided to stop wondering about it.

Daniel encourages me to hitchhike to Green River Community College and back. "All it costs is your thumb." He laughs. "Get it? Your thumb."

"Are you sure it's safe?" I hesitantly ask.

"You'll be fine." Daniel switches tactics. "Maybe I'll come by to pick you up." He gives me a big smile and tilts his head back in my direction.

I take the bus up the hill to the college to be sure I won't be late. On the way back home, I give hitchhiking a try. I walk partway and then hold out my thumb. A man with black hair and a square face pulls up in an old white Toyota sedan. He stops to pick me up. At first, he seems nice, but something is off. His shirt is pressed, but overly bleached. "I'll get out here. Thanks," I say.

"Where do you live?" he asks. We are two miles from my apartment, and I didn't want to tell him.

"I'll just get out here." He starts to slow for a stoplight. I get out of the car while it's still moving. I run behind the nearest apartment complex. The people there assume it's a domestic squabble and let me know when he finally leaves.

I explain what happened. "Don't ever hitchhike," a young man warns. I'll call him Arnold. "Don't you know the Green River Killer had his first kill near the overpass right there?" Arnold points. It is less than one block away. "The Green River Killer started his killing spree only last year. He targets hitchhikers and prostitutes, and he hasn't been caught."

"They said it was prostitutes," a young woman says. The news profiled the victims as prostitutes.

"No, I knew Amina," Arnold says. "She wasn't a prostitute. She was just a hitchhiker." He looks at the young woman and continues. "We heard the struggle, we all called the police, but they couldn't do anything." I walk over to the overpass and look down. I see where it happened, the water, the bank, the rocks, and the open space where Amina struggled against her killer.

I walk to Daniel's house. His parents are standing in the dining room. I ask his parents, "Why wasn't I warned about the Green River Killer?" Viola is alarmed. She looks straight at me, but her eyes dart to Thomas.

Thomas speaks up, "We don't talk about that kind of thing here."

Viola says, "Yes, only pleasant things."

Thomas asks Viola, "One of those victims was a friend of yours, wasn't she?"

Viola responds, "Yes," and sadly looks at the floor. Daniel isn't there, so I walk back home.

Daniel comes by my apartment and asks me to visit him at his house. He walks me back to his bedroom. I look around for a crawl space as I make my way to the end of the hall to his room. No crawl space. I don't have to worry about dead bodies. We don't have sex, but it goes further than I want and it is all about him. As I go to leave, his parents are praying loudly in the living room. The pray is derogatory. Negative energy fills the room. "Is there a back door?" I ask his parents, looking behind me towards the kitchen and not wanting to go through the pulsating black cloud in the living room in front of me.

Thomas says, "Just use the front door." He is looking at me and wondering what is wrong with me.

I sprint across the room and out the front door, closing the screen door, but not closing the house door behind me. I sprint the 0.7 miles home. What are these people? I stay away for a while.

Daniel visits me at my apartment. He asks me to leave my bedroom window unlocked so that he can crawl through. I discuss it with a woman at the college. "Do you want to wake up and find a man standing in your bedroom?" she asks. "Think about it." When Daniel comes around, I insist that he use the front door.

Viola asks her son, Daniel, to invite me to a prayer meeting at the Auburn Free Methodist Church and make sure I come. "What time do you have classes tomorrow?" Daniel asks me.

"My class isn't until 2:45 p.m. on Thursday," I reply. Ironically, it is an Assertiveness Training course. I have work early in the morning cleaning apartments, but I don't mention that.

"My mother wants you to come to a two-hour prayer meeting at the church tonight at seven."

I tell Daniel, "I don't even think your mother likes me."

"It's very important to her that you come to the prayer meeting." He snaps angrily, "Why are you being so selfish? It's only two hours of your life." He changes tactics and nods, looking worried. He continues to insist and beg. "I told her you would come."

I give him a disgusted look. Why was he deciding what I'd do? Then I say, "Fine, I'll go."

"My mother says a lady always carries her purse," he says with a smile as he turns his face towards me and walks out the door. It is the same tense smile he had in the car in the McDonalds parking lot when he smacked the change out of my hands.

After he leaves, Liz asks, "Do you want to go to the prayer meeting?"

"No, but it is only an hour or two." I decided I should be less selfish. "If it makes them happy, I could go."

Liz has a bad feeling about this. I'm hesitant to go to the prayer meeting and she wants to know why. "It's just that I don't like the way they pray," I confess to Liz.

"Just pray your prayer," Liz advises. "They'll never know." I nod.

The time is 6:45 p.m. I usually arrive at places early. I'm cutting this close. It takes fifteen minutes to walk to the church, but I don't want to be there even a minute before. "Should I take my purse?" I look back at Liz, who gives a weak smile. We've already gone over this. Boys carry wallets in their pockets. Girls don't always need their purses. Dan doesn't understand girls. "Oh, I'll only be gone for a couple of hours." I put my purse back on the dining room table and walk out the apartment door, past the blackberry brambles, through the muddy path in the hedge, and down the sidewalk to the Free Methodist Church.

I slip into the pew and kneel on the floor. I pray my prayer until the preacher says, "Amen." The prayer meeting was over. I open my eyes and look over at Viola. She smiles at me. I completed the request.

A girl about my age was standing next to Viola. I hadn't noticed her before. I'll call her Arianna. Arianna asked me, "Do you want a night out?" I look at the time. I have forty-five minutes. We ended early.

I looked at Viola who solemnly nodded. I assumed Arianna was a regular churchgoer. Maybe this was my treat for cooperating. This is a dry church, with no alcohol. I assume Arianna means the Methodist version of a fun night out, you know, girls getting together to play Yahtzee. So I say, "Sure," and we left. I get into her car with her. A man and an older woman are sitting in the front seats. I'll call the older woman Ariel. We sit in the back. We drove for about twenty minutes down Auburn Way S, well past the Piggly Wiggly Supermarket. I was concerned about the time. I told Liz I would be gone for two hours. The prayer meeting was 1.25 hours. That gave me an extra forty-five minutes to have fun. But if we drive south for twenty minutes, there would only be five minutes left to do something and then it would be twenty minutes back home. I was told not to worry. I was driven to the top of the hill where girls were lined up on the side of the road.

Then Ariel announces, "Here we are, Griffin Avenue."

I wonder if Ariel is trying to give us the impression we turned off of SR 164. I ask, "Did we turn?"

Ariel looks back at me and says, "We made a turn."

The driver nods and smiles, "A left, a right, and a left," he answers. We all step out of the car.

Ariel tells me, "Let Arianna go first. She is more mature and knows how to give the man what he wants."

I'm a mouthy teenager who speaks my mind. "I disagree that is more mature."

One of the men cranks his head out the open driver-side window and shouts, "Hey, a girl with a brain. I want her." Ariel shakes her head no.

Ariel nods toward two girls behind her and says, "They will show you what to do." The girl she nods towards has a sad, vacant look on her face as if she doesn't want to be there. Ariel glances at me and goes on to say, "Don't worry about a change of clothes. We'll get you something to wear."

I don't want to be here. I tell her, "I am leaving."

Ariel responds, "I don't know what will happen to you if you leave. We'll take care of you here and give you a place to stay. You aren't wanted where you are now."

I say, "My roommates will be waiting up for me."

Ariel turns to face me and looks stunned. "Roommates?"

A man pulls up and says, "She didn't know why she was here? Is this how you are getting your recruits now?"

Ariel asks Arianna who brought me there. "Didn't you tell her why she was here?" Arianna shrugs and answers, "I thought she kind of knew."

I left on foot. I was in Cross Country in high school and could go nineteen miles with no problem. The man who questioned Ariel about her recruits pulled up in his car and asked me, "Do you want a ride?"

I say, "No thanks. I'll walk. It's mostly downhill." He flashes his police badge and nods, so I got in his car as he glances behind him. Ariel was busy helping a girl into a car and not looking. On the way home, I told him what happened.

"A night on the town where you are never allowed to return to your apartment," the police officer said. He asked if any of the other girls were in a similar situation. I mentioned one of the girls. He said he noticed her too and that there was a safe house he could take her to. He pulled up to Briar Crest Apartments. He looked at the apartment complex, "They don't know you live here. They think you live someplace else. Even if they knew you cleaned ovens for the landlord, they wouldn't have invited you along."

"So, I tell people I clean ovens for my landlord?" He doesn't respond to my question.

"I'm going to find out what is going on." He is resolute. "Don't forget your purse."

"I didn't bring my purse," as I slip out the passenger door.

"Your ID is in your pocket." I didn't answer. I didn't have my ID. If he wanted to see it, I'd retrieve it from my apartment. He didn't say anything more and drove away.

I came home and saw my purse open on the dining room table. Liz and Carla were in the living room and the lights were low. I hadn't lied to the older woman after all. My roommates were waiting up for me. You said you were going to be gone for two hours. It's been four hours," Carla starts in and is impatient.

Liz says, concerned, "We called Dan and he said you went out and said, 'She took her purse with her didn't she?' We looked through your purse and nothing is missing."

"Oh, so that is why my purse is open. You said I didn't need to bring it."

Liz responds, "I guess you won't be going to any more prayer meetings."

I'm exasperated, "I won't be doing 'any more' of a lot of things." Carla says, "I have work in the morning."

Liz adds, "I have class. We are going to bed."

As I was getting ready to clean apartments, I stopped to talk with the landlord and pick up an apartment key. I asked the landlord if the police had called. He says, "No why?"

"I got a ride home from the police last night," I inform.

He chuckles. "It's never good when you get a ride home from the police."

"A girl at the church asked if I wanted to go for a night out and I was expecting the Methodist version."

He says, "You don't need to tell me what happened. I can guess."

Later Daniel talked with my landlord. After Daniel heard the conversation I had with my landlord, he says solemnly, "Oh right, you were expecting the Methodist version of a night out."

The landlord got a look of scrutiny on his face. He says to me about Daniel, "He had something to do with it."

"What do you know about it?" I ask.

"Just what you told me." He left it at that and went back to his office.

When Daniel invited me to his parents' house again, Viola was shocked to see me and embarrassed. She was so pale her skin looked purple and her gray hair looked dark. She said in a gasp, with her hand to her throat, "It didn't work. You're still here." She was frozen in position.

Daniel walked me home and wanted to know who I had told. I said I told my roommates. He was worried, then said, "They...they must have thought you were nuts. I'll have to talk with them."

After his talk, my roommates told me, "We are worried and very scared." They didn't explain why.

"Your mother didn't even apologize," I explained the reason for the breakup.

Daniel continued to beg for me to date him again. "She didn't know," he insisted. We stopped by the house. Viola is sitting at the dining room table. Daniel leans over from across the table and says, "Mother, tell her you didn't know."

"I...," Viola started to say.

"Enough!" Thomas yelled from the living room. As Daniel and I are walking out, I hear Thomas say to Viola, "You knew she was going to become a missing person and she would have been missed."

Later the Auburn Police Department called. I told him about Viola's reaction like she had seen a ghost. "I'll bet," he affirmed. The police detective completed his investigation. He explained that while Viola was grocery shopping, she had complained to a woman at Auburn's Main Street Market about me and portrayed me as an unwelcome houseguest. The woman promised Viola she would take me in and Viola would never see me again. So, Viola invited a girl to the church to intercept me. The police told me not to go to Thomas and Viola Bondehagen's house anymore. "They didn't get any money for you. I checked." He didn't indicate how he checked. He said, "There aren't any girls missing from the Auburn Free Methodist Church." From the detective's perspective, it was a wrap.

Karen Roberts

FLAGS

1986

I'm sitting in the group counseling session at Domestic Abuse Women's Network. I'm quietly circling items on the worksheets. One worksheet is for recognizing red flags. The other worksheet is for types of abuse and their progression. Others are talking, as they pass an object around the room. The person with the object is the one who has a chance to talk. When it comes to my turn, I pass this time. I'm concentrating on the worksheets. After the counseling session, two women verbally attack me, telling me I was rude for not listening to the others. They confront me about visiting with my husband outside of the building last week. I'm confused at first and then realize they are referring to one of my neighbors playing Frisbee outside. "That wasn't my husband. It was a neighbor," I explained.

"Why were you talking to him?" they confronted again.

"I hadn't seen him for a while. I was worried about him," I explained further.

"Karen, go outside," the facilitator requests. I head out the door.

As I am leaving, I hear the group facilitators explain to the two women, "The worksheets are part of our plan for her. She leaves the worksheets here so her husband doesn't find them. It's for her safety."

The next week I'm at the group counseling session again. The facilitators explain, "The two women won't be coming back. They didn't really need to be here. They've promised not to tell anyone where we are located. Karen, you passed when it was your turn. They didn't hear you share. They must have been disappointed."

One of the group members commented, "I thought it was interesting that they verbally attacked Karen. There were plenty of members in the group not listening." The facilitators nodded.

2021

At our last family reunion, I bring up that Daniel had caught a venereal disease from his mother. I know what Viola was doing with Daniel. I wondered how Viola would have contracted it. She was a churchgoing woman and had been married to one man for a long time. My mother reminded me that Viola referred to me as, "well-dated." She informed me that Daniel told them that I had worked as a prostitute. It takes them from 1986 to 2021 to tell me this and give me an opportunity to respond. That's thirty-five years!

My father tells my mother, "Dan said that is why he hated her so much." My father turns to face me and accuses me, "You were working as a prostitute and having men wear condoms."

"Condoms," I say with the most discussed look on my face. How gross!

My mother yells at my father, "Clark, don't you know your daughter better than that?" She never yells at my father, but she was now. "Why would he have married her if he hated her?"

"He felt obligated to," my father says.

"That doesn't make sense," my mother says.

Later at work, "Have you ever had sex for money?" one of the area managers asks me at a group business meeting.

I wonder why I'm being asked this question. It keeps coming up. I thought I knew the reason. At first, I thought it had something to do with the human trafficking up north, admission of guilt for those involved. Then I thought it was about a girl from Wuhan City who asks my boyfriend out to dinner and sticks him with the check. But now I'm thinking I was wrong. I've always been wrong and the question is about something else. "Of course, I haven't," I say. For the first time, I wonder if this is in the file the FBI flagged.

"We are trying to be discreet," another area manager says.

"I'm not interested in discreet." I make this clear. "I want transparency. I want to get to the bottom of things."

November 2021

A state worker shows up at my work. I can spot them. She is standing on the manager's side of the desk without wearing a vest. I'll call her Ashley. I should have ushered her out, but I was distracted with my work. The subject of Viola enters into the conversation. Ashley comments, "You know, some of those Avon ladies weren't always Avon ladies. They were just going door to door selling something." This was a missing piece of a puzzle that made everything click. I would never have thought of that. By "Avon Lady" they meant prostitute.

"That means the file the FBI flagged is about Viola," I say. "It all fits; raised to be a homemaker, poor inner-city, the crying to get attention, the addiction to phenobarbital as a pleasure drug, the work as a prostitute, making up stories, the file is about her. Ms. Nightingale, the investigator, must have contacted Viola Bondehagen. She must have thought Viola was my mother."

"And Viola didn't correct her," Ashley pointed out.

"Viola didn't know me, so she described herself," I said. "I had very little contact with Viola."

"She lived in California," Ashley inserted.

"Yes, but in addition to that, the police told me not to visit her," I say.

"Why is that?" Ashley asks with curiosity.

I explain what the police detective told me and add, "Viola was trying to get rid of me, because I was dating her son. She was complaining about me to a woman at the grocery store, and the woman said she would take me in. Viola expected to never see me again. She knew I would become a missing person."

"No," Ashley said. "They wouldn't have accepted you with such little information. She knew them. They accepted you because they knew her and trusted her."

December 2021

Another arrives at my work. I'll call her Augustine. "I sense you are pregnant. There is a life force coming from you," she says to me, gesturing towards her abdomen.

"Show me your badge," I demand. "And don't put your thumb over the picture."

"Karen, I'll handle this," says the night shift AM. I leave to finish my work.

"Actually, I don't have a badge," Augustine says, expecting the AM will understand.

"Oh, you don't have a badge," the AM says, nodding and smiling. "Isn't that interesting?"

"I was paid to be here," Augustine defends as if that will help her case. I never saw her again.

Two weeks later, two more state workers arrived. I'll call them Avery and Axel. They try hard to fit in, but never really "get it." They sat on boxes of tape, something no one would ever do.

"They told us what happened," Avery says.

"Does that make it easier to talk about it?" Axel asks.

"Do you remember when you were asked that?" Avery prodded. "And you wondered who told?"

"I didn't wonder 'who told,'" I corrected. "I wondered who was 'they.'" I explained. "'Who told' illustrates understanding and some agreement, whereas 'who is they' illustrates complete confusion."

Axel says to Avery, "I've never seen that backfire so badly."

Avery says to Axel, "She was told to say that." Avery asks me, "What was that about anyway?"

"I have no idea. To this day, I have no idea," I answer. "Obviously, you know more about it than I do."

"They tried to use that as a ploy and it backfired," Axel says. "They didn't know what it is about."

"It's just a lead-in to get the person to talk." One of the packers accuses, "You're obtaining information under false pretenses."

Avery asks me, "How do you know they had false information?"

"All of their information was wrong," I explain.

Axel says, "There is a problem with the word 'they.'"

"Well, yes, there is," I answer. "It makes no sense. I was attacked by one person from behind. There was no 'they'." I'm referring to an assault in 1990.

Avery says, "The police told us what happened."

"That makes no sense either," I say. "The police were prosecuting a fraud case in conjunction with the assault case. They wanted to treat the fraud case as primary. They charged him with assault and indecent liberties. But they were waiting on the fraud charges. The charges for fraud and embezzlement came, but that took a while. By that time, he'd left the state. Or as the police report reads, 'evaded Washington State authorities.'"

1990

I was attacked in my bedroom from behind. Despite all my efforts, I couldn't get that man off me. This wasn't normal. I saw gray fuzz after I was hit on the back of the head, then navy blue, then he was gone. The blue was the same color as my sleeping bag. My sleeping bag is lying on my bunk, undisturbed without even a wrinkle. But it was also the same blue as the sweatpants of the man who just threatened me, the one who threatened me to be silent. I, of all people, should know better than to leave the bedroom window open. Why did that come into my head? What past event is my brain referring to? I needed to get out of there. Gather up my things, gather up my passengers. I was responsible for their safety. Barry was one of my passengers. "Those guys are a bunch of perverts," he said as I was throwing luggage into the trunk of the state car. "I worked as an investigative reporter for the *Omak and Okanogan County Chronicle*. I sat in on those court hearings. They hired that guy knowing he was a sex offender."

Barry informs me that our missing passenger is in the other bunkhouse. There is a second bunkhouse? I sprint across the lawn. "I've never seen anyone run so fast," Barry says. I finally locate my missing passenger. She decided to take a ride home with another group without informing me. She wants to take the Bremerton Ferry to Seattle and then go back home. Wasted minutes, damn it. Now the roads are blocked. The Rhododendron Festival Fun Run is taking place, a 5K and 10K. We can't get out. The men standing around as Security aren't cops. Crap! Who designed this place? The only phone is in a building that is locked. Joan knows the way out. She has to get to work. We'll follow behind her. We cut through parking lot after parking lot. Joan knows what she's doing. I just need to keep up. Now open road, back to SR 16. I know the way from here. At this point, I'll just get everyone home safely and then contact the police.

I stop to visit the pastor at his house after dropping off the state car. He is pastor at the Assembly of God church. "Just know," Pastor Murphy says, "it's going to be a difficult road. People don't want to accept their own mortality. They would rather blame the victim."

"I might have a legal responsibility to report," I admit. "These men work with the public school district."

"Sheesh, I wish you good luck," Murphy says. "And I'll be praying for you."

Think Karen think; what all did he say? There is too much information to even write it down. I need a Dictaphone. I was to deliver a message from the Special Education Director in Puyallup at the next committee meeting. I'll wait until then. I need to gather up more information and be organized. It won't do any good to make a report like this. I didn't even see his face, just the blue of his sweatpants.

I meet with Professor Frank Carlson, my SWEA advisor. He confirms I have a legal responsibility to report. He suggests going through Affirmative Action. This turns out to be a bad idea.

1991

Ms. Nightingale used old AT&T records to find who I might be related to. She thought Viola Bondehagen was my mother. She reasoned the relationship of mother explained why we had the same last name when I was eighteen years old. But Ms. Nightingale didn't tell me she called Viola. She didn't tell me she was asking about Viola. She just used the generic word "mother" in her questions to me. "Your relationship with your mother is what defines you," she said. She asked me, "Did you marry your brother?"

"No," I responded. I was trying to figure out who Ms. Nightingale would assume is my brother.

I had no idea why Ms. Nightingale asked the question. From my response, Ms. Nightingale assumed I was never married. Was Daniel Bondehagen contacted by Ms. Nightingale? Did Daniel claim I was his sister? It wouldn't be the first time.

Ms. Read wrote up a complaint and attached my name to it. When I wrote, "I was married to Dan," Ms. Read assumed I had never been married and the statement was a sign of mental illness. Ms. Read also assumed I made a complaint against a professor. "The professor proposed marriage during classroom instruction" was the complaint Ms. Read wrote. Every syllable of that complaint is wrong. It isn't my witness statement. I objected to my name being attached to it, but my objections were ignored. I had one class to complete for my education degree, just my student teaching, and I wasn't able to take it. Professor Dan Fennerty assumed I was obsessed with him because I said I was married to Dan. The professor was convinced he was the Dan mentioned. There was no way to correct him.

The report I was making was about Mr. Clark, the man with the navy-blue sweatpants at the Rhododendron Festival. This was completely lost. This was supposed to be a pit stop. A quick task to complete. Then finally I would be able to make the complaint I had been trying to make ever since my car was blocked in at the Rhododendron Fun Run.

Finally, there was progress. Rick Wilson who examines fingerprints for the Washington State Patrol found something. "I have two fingerprint cards on my desk right now, both for a William C. Clark. One was submitted by Rochester. The other was submitted by Westport." A public records search showed there was only one William C. Clark in the Office of Professional Practices database with a valid teaching certificate number. The other William Clark was a fake using the real William Clark's credentials. Which was which?

Rick asked me to locate someone who was in administrative credentials at Central Washington University in 1982. I check and read it was Dr. Conrad. Is Dr. Conrad on campus? Yes! I'm in luck. I call the education department secretary to set up a meeting. Head of Education Department Dr. Conrad says, "Tell me about this complaint you have against a professor."

I strongly assert, "I don't have a complaint against a professor. I'm here to discuss something that happened in 1982."

Dr. Conrad says, "I'm not going to rehash anything that happened in 1982. I want to discuss what is happening now."

I assert, "If you are not willing to discuss 1982, then there is no reason for this meeting."

Dr. Conrad says, putting his foot down, "There is no reason for this meeting."

That didn't go as expected. "Why are all these people here?"

Dr. Conrad answers, "This is a panel." I give a bewildered look and leave.

[Axel interrupts again. "So you already knew this man was a fraud?"

I respond, "Yes, the Washington State Patrol already found two distinct fingerprint cards. But there was only one William C. Clark in the Office of Professional Practices database with a valid teaching certificate number. You need two teaching certificate numbers for two distinct fingerprints or one teaching certificate number for one fingerprint card." I check to make sure he is following this. He nods. "The man who examines the fingerprint cards asked me to meet with someone who was in administrative credentials at CWU back in 1982. Unfortunately, Dr. Conrad was just promoted to Head of the Education Department; and he thought the meeting was about his new position instead of his old one."

"And he never wanted to know the reason you were there to talk about 1982?" Axel asks.

"No," I answer. "Now they are trying to make the fraud out to be something I learned about later, but it wasn't. The fraud was first."]

The CWU attorney, Ms. Kulik, submits to Halverson & Applegate a request that I do not speak with a list of about 200 people. None of these people on the list had ever requested "no contact." There is no rationale for the "no contact." The protection order was incomplete. There was a note to "see attached" with nothing attached. The police could not serve the order.

1992

Central Washington Comprehensive Mental Health psychiatrist Dr. Kramer asks, "Tell me about your marriage to Dan."

I respond, "We were married in King County." I mention the county so he can check marriage certificates in public records.

Dr. Kramer interrupts, "Is that where you met the professor?"

Wondering why he is switching to questions about the professor, I answer, "Almost, I was planning to go to the movie *Gorky Park* at the Magnolia Theater, but I couldn't get off work. That same weekend, he went on a double date to the movie."

Dr. Kramer asks, "So you were on a double date?"

I correct him, "No, I couldn't get off work."

Back to the Present

Axel interjects, "Dr. Kramer was evaluating you based on your complaint. But he never asked you about your complaint. Instead, he asked you about your marriage and a professor." He laughs as he puts it together. He focuses on my reaction.

"Yes, that makes sense. We were supposed to discuss my complaint. It was so confusing. I hadn't asked for the meeting. The prosecuting attorney set it up without giving even one word as to why." But I also didn't have a chance to talk about my marriage to Dan, other than the county we were married in.

"That was an interesting story about the double date," Axel compliments.

"Oh, thank you," I respond. "Yes, that was interesting. Dan Fennerty was going on a double date with his wife, his best friend, and his best friend's wife on the same weekend I was planning to go on a double date with my fiancé, his best friend, and his best friend's wife. And we would have gone to the same movie at the same theater."

"Only you couldn't get off work," Axel finishes.

I nod. "I had worked nine days straight and really needed the time off. They had to go without me."

"So you didn't meet the professor in King County," Axel clarifies. I shake my head no.

"I studied this thing like crazy. I'm poking all kinds of holes in your story," Avery brags. "You wouldn't have walked home if they drove you twenty minutes. You would have taken the bus."

I'm getting upset. "I didn't have my purse with me. I didn't have money for the bus. I didn't know where I was or the bus system there. I wouldn't have known what bus to wait for. And I wouldn't have been able to stand and wait at a bus stop without being grabbed. All I knew is that I wasn't going to be allowed to go home, ever."

He continued to argue, "You would have taken your purse with you to bring your ID and money for the night out."

"I was told I was going to a prayer meeting," I argue. "I didn't need my purse. This was a Wednesday night. I only tithe on Sunday. Why would I need my ID or money for a night out? I was barely eighteen."

"Don't you know how to have fun?" he mocks.

"I do know how to have fun, a different kind of fun. I was expecting Methodist girls playing Yahtzee. And Yahtzee isn't a euphemism for something else. Yahtzee is just Yahtzee." How can I get him to understand. I'm learning his nature. "Your type of fun would be a nightmare to me."

He is finally getting it. "I was thinking she was there voluntarily," Avery said to Axel. "This was a felony. 'No ID' shows intent."

My supervisor says, "I can't believe how many times a week she has to address this."

Explaining my supervisor's comment, "There was a person here earlier this week who was trying to get me to believe I'm pregnant. Usually, these come in twos, the first trying to get me to believe I'm pregnant and the second who evaluates my mental competency for thinking I might be pregnant."

Avery looks down and reads. "That is further down on our list."

"Did you notice who submitted the file to us?" Axel asked.

"No," Avery admitted.

"It was anonymous. That is the first thing I check," Axel said. "You told me we were going, so I decided it would be best if I went with you. I'm looking for where she is confused. Everything in the file is from the perspective of Daniel Bondehagen and his family."

"I'm still trying to wrap my head around the idea that this isn't about Dan Fennerty," Avery admits.

Axel looks back at me and nudges Avery on the arm with his elbow. "The best stories come from real life."

Referring to 1983, I continue to explain, "An Auburn undercover police officer asked me if I wanted a ride. I told him it was downhill and I would just walk."

[Axel interrupts. "You said they drove you twenty minutes south. You may not have been in Auburn anymore. It may not have been the Auburn Police Department. Where could it have been?"

"I would think Enumclaw, but I don't know. Maybe Black Diamond, but I'm not sure where that is, maybe Puyallup, maybe."

"You said, 'Puyallup'?" He looked up from his paper.

"Probably not that far south. We drove south past the Piggly Wiggly Market and kept on the same road. That is why I figured I'd be able to make it back, even on foot." Looking at a map, twenty minutes would put me in downtown Enumclaw. A walk back would have taken five hours. The state worker nods.]

1983

On Sunday, Daniel runs up to me at church, gasping for breath. "Hey, We... take your place... invited her to dinner." He laughs. "I had to say she was my sister." Then gives a boyish shrug of his shoulders.

I look at him completely noncomprehending. What does he mean by, "my place"?

He is disappointed. "I thought you would be happy."

A man at the church comes up to me. He is tall with black hair. I haven't seen him before. But I haven't seen any of these people before. I ask him, "What did he say?"

The man with black hair says, "I was going to ask you the same question." I said, thinking out loud, "His sister lives in Oregon."

The man parrots my response, "His sister lives in Oregon." Either he didn't hear what Daniel said or he isn't saying. He is no help.

[Axel interjects, "He probably didn't want to add to your statement."

"I don't know," I hadn't thought of that before. I always assume people are at a church because they attend.]

Another man in the back of the church yells, "… didn't come home. Does anyone here know anything?"

I'm thinking. I'm here. I came home. Daniel grabs me and steers me away, claiming I have mental issues. Later when we are alone, I ask him, "What did you mean by 'We invited her to dinner and I had to say she was my sister'?"

"I thought you would be happy that it wasn't you," he said, still disappointed.

"You don't understand me. I mean, you completely don't understand me." I had a bad feeling.

"She wanted to go," Daniel says.

I wonder to myself, go where?

"What did you do? Why were they here? We've never had someone ask so many questions before." Daniel is insistent and angry, "You must have done something."

I wonder, what does he mean by "before"? Why would there be a "before"? I don't answer. I don't even give a facial expression. I don't ask any more questions.

At the Auburn Free Methodist Church, one of the college students noticed that Daniel was stalking me. She had a friend tell me. "She wants to talk with you in the kitchen." We talked in the kitchen and I told her what I knew. Daniel came around to locate me. She turned to her friend and asked. "How much time did we have?"

"Five minutes," her friend answers.

"That's not normal," then quietly she adds, "They are protecting Viola Bondehagen."

1984

Daniel and I move to an apartment in Kent, Washington, which I paid for. As I'm unpacking my things, Daniel finds my gloves and looks closely at them. "Your gloves are dirty," he said. "You can tell where they've been. You need to buy new ones."

"I want to tell where they've been." I explain, "They were my grandmother's gloves. They were on her hands, in her flower bed, in her dirt, weeding her roses. I want to remember that."

"She gave you her used gloves?" he asks.

"Yes, after showing me how to weed the roses." I say, "It is sentimental dirt."

Thomas and Viola are planning a move to California. "They've always wanted to live in California. They checked and they only need $10,000 for the down payment. They felt God told them to do it," Daniel explained. "We should go to church with them a few times before they leave. We will be getting married there soon."

[Axel questions, "How were they able to go from barely making the bills and needing for Viola to work as an 'Avon Lady' to buying a house in California?"

"I don't know. They sold their house in Auburn. Maybe that paid for it?"

"Property is more expensive in California," he pondered.

"Was it back then? This was 1984." Axel doesn't answer and continues to write. Axel looks up at me and explains, "Viola, a satellite call girl, was required

to make regular payments to her contacts. This means you may have been abducted in lieu of payment. And they are still trying to extract payment for your freedom."

Thankfully a packer came up to me and asked for help with his tape dispenser. I left to go fix the jammed machine. "It's okay," I assured him. "You're more important than that conversation." After Avery and Axel left, memories continued to come back.]

After the church service. "She came back!" Voices of excitement are happening throughout the church.

Daniel laughs with delight. "She has been out there this whole time." He turns to look at me.

I have a look of concern on my face, which he misreads, "You're right. We need to get going." We swiftly exit the back way directly to the parking lot and drive straight home. After he calls his parents, he says, "They were expecting us to stay for dinner, but they understood." Less worried, he says, "I checked with my parents. We can continue to go to the same church, just not as often. It doesn't matter now, because they are moving to California anyways." I don't follow what he is saying.

At the wedding, the college friend said, "Daniel has stopped stalking you. He has you where he wants you." She is concerned; her voice is low and shaky. She smiles and adds, "I think it is good that Thomas and Viola are moving to Banning, California." The wedding cake is gone before I had a piece. My grandmother ran off with the cake top for good luck. That is six pieces we had counted to serve that are now missing. She promises to return the cake top for our one-year anniversary. Our wedding night is a bust. All Daniel wants to do is watch *National Lampoon's Summer Vacation*. I cry in the bathroom. The next night is no better.

Thomas and Viola Bondehagen meet with my parents at their home in Battle Ground. Viola gives Daniel a kiss on the lips. He said, "Hey, I used

to give my mother a kiss every day; and I won't be seeing her for a while."
He is now twenty-five years old.

After we got back home to our apartment in Kent, Daniel decided what we should do with our wedding presents. He took them over to K-Mart to sell them, hoping to get a good deal and knowing K-Mart would take them without a receipt or a hassle. I didn't know what Daniel was planning. Some of our presents were sold. Then they looked at my face. "They take one look at your face and stop," Daniel said. "This shouldn't be happening."

I called the Auburn Police Department to check whether it was okay to help Thomas and Viola Bondehagen pack up their things for the move to California. The Auburn Police Department said this was okay and there may not have been a reason to restrict me before. I was sure there was, but I didn't argue. I went to Thomas and Viola's house and boxed up their things. I was relieved to see them go. They told Daniel he could take the swivel rocker and asked him to return the telephone they had rented. Daniel told me to do it for him. He was leaving for Seattle. I told him I didn't know where to return the telephone. He told me the phone store was along the river and I wouldn't miss it. I drove around and couldn't find the store. I never offered or agreed to return their phone. So, I got angry and threw the phone out the car window onto the grass. Thomas and Viola received a charge for the missing phone.

At the apartment I'm looking for something to wear, I spot his red tennis shoes. "What size are these?" I ask, holding up the shoes.

"Size 12, I usually wear size 11, but those are size 12," he says. "I have big feet to go with my monkey arms."

"Can I borrow your red tennis shoes and wear them at work?" I ask.

"What for?" he asks.

"We are having a carnival day at work. I'm dressing as a clown and making balloon animals," I say with delight. "I already bought the balloons. I decided not to do face makeup and just wear the nose."

"You already had a nose?" he asks.

"Our church youth group dressed as clowns and made balloon animals at a Fourth of July celebration."

"Great," he said with exasperation. "I married a clown. Sure, you can borrow the shoes."

I come out of the bathroom. "How do I look?" I ask.

"Somehow it doesn't bother me," he says. "Maybe because it is my wife." He smiles but doesn't kiss me. I don't understand why. I'm not wearing any facial makeup. There is no makeup to smear.

Daniel takes me into Seattle and shows me the homeless there. "It was explained to me that the mental institutions were too crowded," he says, detailing the problem. "So they put them out on the streets." He encourages me to look around. "They used to pick them up and put them in jail, but that was giving them a warm place to sleep and a free meal." I see the smiling faces of the men standing by and I warmly smile back. "There are just too many of them." Daniel looks back at me. "You see the problem, don't you?" I nod. "I want to help them," Daniel tells me. "Once every other week, stay in Seattle on Sunday after church, and feed the homeless. I'll take them to McDonalds. You can stay home." I appreciate this man. He is a much better Christian than I am.

About a week later, when I am cleaning, I look for the red shoes. Daniel said, "I threw them away. I couldn't look at them anymore."

Daniel was talking with his mother on the phone. "She wants to talk to you," he said and handed me the phone.

"Work is going well. I dressed as a clown for our carnival," I say to her. "Daniel is feeding the homeless in Seattle. He is taking them to McDonalds."

"Oh no," she exclaims, "not McDonalds."

"Give me the phone back." He grabs it from my hands. "She is just confused. It's okay. It's okay." After he hangs up, he says, "You upset her. I can't let you talk with her on the phone ever again."

I'm the one who pays the phone bill. But then I really didn't want to talk with his mother anyway. I assume I understand her objection. I encourage Daniel to serve hot soup for the homeless instead.

Later I got a call from the Kent police, "We noticed you married Daniel Bondehagen."

"Yes, I did," I explained that I had stayed away from Thomas and Viola as they requested. "I didn't go back to his parent's house after you said not to. I only went to help them move to California. They are no longer in the area. I thought that would help."

"He asked you to marry him and you said, 'Yes'?" the officer asks, almost in disbelief.

"I wasn't that enthusiastic." Remembering the conversation and the used Kleenex in my hand.

"It's just that Viola tried to have you abducted and Daniel would have been an accomplice. We may not be able to protect you."

We go to Des Moines for the day. It is a cool day in early autumn, but it is bright and sunny. I packed a lunch. At the end of the evening, we stood to watch the boats on the pier. It was a lovely trip. On the way home, I spot a hardware store and decide to buy plumbing supplies to fix the leak under the kitchen sink. I need a washer and plumber's tape. I pull into the parking lot. "I'm going to stop at the hardware store," I announce.

Daniel is squirming in his seat, like a fish. "Don't stop here, not at the hardware store," he pleads.

I pull into a parking spot anyway. "Do you want to come in with me?" I ask.

He gives me a mortified look, yells, "No. No," and ducks down in the seat. I walk in to buy my supplies and I'm out again in less than five minutes.

"You just went straight in there," Daniel accuses.

"Of course, I went straight in there," I respond. "I don't want to bother the apartment manager if I can fix it myself."

"I thought you were going to turn around and drive out," Daniel says.

"I'm driving out now. Are you like this towards all hardware stores?" I ask, "Or just this one?" He didn't answer my question.

"Didn't you notice the manager looking out the window?" he asks. "We had a nice day together," he says, "and you end it with this."

Later in the fall, we got together with Ross and Bonnie for a Dungeons & Dragons game. Ross had sandy brown curly hair, medium height, and thin. He was an education major at the college until he was expelled. He had submitted a poster called, "Naughty Bits," which were small cut-out pieces from pornography magazines pasted into a collage. Bonnie was a psychology major and worked at the daycare as a Lead Teacher. They both had a great sense of humor.

Ross was the dungeon master. He helped me create a character. The game was to be easy. But Daniel and his other D&D friend decided to play damsels in distress and wait for me and Bonnie to come to save them. I had to risk everything to rescue us out of there. I saved Bonnie and was told I could save one more. I rescued my horse instead of one of the male players. "You have to save us. We are the ones who have the map of where the treasure is." I left the players with the treasure map to die in the castle. It was a quiet ride home.

At the apartment, Daniel yanked me out of the middle of my shower, when I was soaped up and ready to rinse and made me stand there in the bathroom shivering while he took his complete shower before I would be allowed to rinse off the soap. He was exerting complete control.

Sometimes he would sit in the corner and repeatedly smack himself in the head. When I tried to distract him from the destructive behavior, he would go after me hitting and kicking, arms and legs beating me over and over.

I had made a mistake marrying him. It was embarrassing. If there was any hope of him working as a pastor, I needed to protect his reputation. This was my conundrum.

A visit to Planned Parenthood confirmed that I had a sexually transmitted disease. I asked how this was possible. Daniel and I were both virgins. The Planned Parenthood practitioner stated, "I believe you, but I don't believe your husband."

Daniel tells me, "My mother would rub her juices on my underwear first out of the dryer so that I could have the smell of a woman as a special treat. And I'd just put them on that way." He stops to remember. "My mom was so flustered when she caught a venereal disease. But I told her I was fine." In response to my disgusted reaction, he exclaimed, "I was expecting you to understand."

SOLD

It is painful to admit this. I wasn't only sold into prostitution by my husband; I was sold twice, to his mother's "contacts" in Auburn and again in Seattle. I thought possibly to those who sold sex to the churchgoers outside of the United Methodist Church, but no, those were too up-scale. The second time it was to the group that had prostitutes wait in the middle bay outside of the Seattle Public Library. After these failed attempts, my ex-husband continues to contact my parents for money. In the mess that was going on in his head, he really thought that I worked as a prostitute. That is what his mother, the "Avon Lady," told him when she "explained some things" to him. I never understood what they were talking about. They spoke English, but it was a whole different language.

Daniel receives a call from Thomas, "Your mom doesn't have the contacts in Banning that she had in Auburn. You'll need to get money from your wife." I'm nineteen years old and I'm expected to put a new husband through an expensive college. I didn't sign up for this.

My husband asks me, "Would you have sex for $5?"

"No," I respond with a voice of disgust.

"Would you have sex for $1,000?" I pause. He roars with laughter. "We've already established what you are. Now we are just haggling on the price."

I'm taken aside by another woman and I explain, "Any disgusting man would offer $5 to have sex with me. Only my husband would offer $1,000. He's the only one who would regard it as that valuable. And it is my husband who is asking the question."

"That's beautiful," she says. "If your husband were to offer you $1,000 for sex, of course, you would say 'Yes.' You should explain that to him."

"He just likes to joke," I say.

We visit Seattle and the Dungeons & Dragons player comes up to me for sex. I turn him down. He says, "Your husband is still trying to have you get the treasure you have no interest in." Some people standing nearby and listening in asked me about it.

I respond with irritation, "Well, he knows that I'm married." They asked more questions, but I refused to answer.

"Heavenly Father," I pray at the dining room table.

Daniel slams his fist down and the silverware jumps to a new position. "Say 'God.' He knows who He is. Besides you might be offending Him." Daniel closes his eyes and expects me to pray with his guidelines.

I argue, "I think it is better to be specific." Shouldn't we clarify who we are praying to?

Didn't Jesus teach us how to pray, "Our Father who art in heaven"?

But I comply, partially. In my head, I start with, "Our Father," then aloud I say, "God" just to avoid having the silverware jump to the floor. [I was so relieved when I joined the Unity Church years later and every prayer started with "Mother, Father, God." That was what I silently prayed, well, at least the "Father, God" part, and finally I could pray it out loud with people smiling.]

Later I call up Seattle Pacific University. I want to know if they are teaching about Satan in their theology degree. The Theology Department secretary answers the phone and wants to know why I'm calling and then hangs up. I'm frustrated. A man is listening in on my phone call and understands why I need answers. "It is good that you are praying 'Our Father,' but just once listen to what your husband prays."

So I try his advice. My husband's prayer is okay, but it isn't energizing. It doesn't make me feel good. After the meal, I sit down in the living room to silently pray my prayer. My husband grabs a pillow and whacks me in the head. "What are you doing?"

"I'm praying. I didn't have a chance to pray earlier. Besides, didn't you say that we need to be praying constantly?" And deliver us from evil. Deliver us from evil.

We finally had a chance to get together with old college friends in Auburn. In the kitchen, the hostess said, "We haven't had a chance to talk since the wedding."

A man walked in, he heard part of the conversation and went into the other room and announced, "Karen was telling us about her night in the city." He was shushed and the hostess told us the party was ending so we'd leave.

When I got home, she called me on the phone to make sure I was okay. I said, "Everything is all right."

Daniel was listening and silently and slowly, creeping closer, looking intent. I hung up the phone. "I wanted to talk with her," he said.

I replied, "She called to talk to me."

After I was in a sound sleep, he picked me up and threw me down hard onto the floor next to the bed. I lay there weeping while he went back to sleep. I thought his physical abuse was over, and I was wrong. I waited for him to leave the house and crawled to the phone. The operator connected me to the Kent Police Department. "A friend called to check on me...." The officer wanted to know her name and then called me back. I explained the situation and was encouraged to work with the Domestic Abuse Women's Network (DAWN). I didn't know what that was.

Karen Roberts

1985

I let my husband use my car. I rode the bus to work. After work, I waited in the third bay outside of the Seattle Public Library for Daniel to pick me up. A police officer came up to me and asked who I was waiting for. "My husband," I answered.

Daniel pulls up in my car. He looks out the passenger window, smiles, and nods. The police officer leans over and looks at him. "He doesn't look like your husband." Daniel's smile fades and is replaced with fear. I open the glove box and show the officer my vehicle registration and my ID and explain the change of my last name. I give him my current address and telephone number. In the middle bay, two teenagers are looking over at us and talking. I overhear part of their conversation. The police officer continues, "I received a call about two prostitutes waiting outside of the Seattle Public Library."

The woman standing next to me speaks up. She is a middle-aged housewife and is now offended that she is assumed to be a prostitute. "You come after us as prostitutes because we are waiting for our husbands?" The police officer looks at her and rolls his eyes.

"You come after us as prostitutes when there are two prostitutes right there in the middle bay?" I accused.

"Oh, I thought they were teenagers waiting for their dad," said the police officer, straightening up and taking a sharper look. "I don't usually make this kind of mistake."

I get into the car with Daniel. Daniel says, "I'm trying to understand what they could have gotten ahold of. I would have given the police officer the wrong address and telephone number. That is what I thought you would do. Now we need to go straight home."

We always go straight home. Why would today be any different? It is a quiet ride home. When we get home, Daniel is pacing the floor. He finally takes a walk outside.

As soon as he leaves, the phone rings. It is the Kent Police Department, "Is your husband gone?"

I reply, "Yes, he's gone." I look out the window. Is a police officer watching the apartment?

The officer goes on to say, "Your husband didn't give the reaction the officer was looking for. The officer expected your husband to be indignant. Or say, 'How could you think that about my wife?'" Now I understand.

Daniel comes back into the apartment, "I knew they were going to call." He is furious. He picks up the phone and dials the Seattle Police Department to call them back. (Seattle, not Kent.) Daniel complains, "My wife won't let me drive the car anymore." They laugh.

Daniel tries to take money out of my savings account at the cash machine and it won't work. I had added his name to my checking account and regretted it. He went through my money like water and left the checking account overdrawn. There was no explanation of where he spent the money. This was usually the money I was paid for helping out my grandfather on the dairy farm. Daniel takes me with him to the Seattle branch where I opened the savings account. He passes on the male bank clerk and zeros in on the female bank clerk demanding that his name be added to the savings account and accusing the bank of making a mistake. I'm behind him shaking my head. The female bank clerk doesn't notice, but the bank manager does. The bank manager offers to freeze both my checking and savings accounts. I'm grateful to him. We walk out. Daniel wonders what kind of bank is this.

Daniel puts his body behind me and requests, "Show me how you would break my ribs." I show the defense move. "God," he gasps, "I need to get further back."

We move from our studio apartment to a one-bedroom apartment in the same apartment complex. This part of the apartment complex has a main office and a pool. My mother and grandmother decided to come to visit. My grandmother has a special treat. She wants to reupholster the furniture in my apartment. "Does she know how to reupholster?" I ask, doubtful this is going to work.

"Oh, yes," my mother responds. "She is very good at it. Just go to the fabric store and pick out the upholstery you want."

"Do they have upholstery at the fabric store?" I ask. I remain doubtful this will work.

"It's in the back of the store," my mother informs.

I assume she is wrong, but sure enough, the upholstery is there on tall hangers. I find neutral colors to replace the mustard yellow sofa and the seafoam green chair, chocolate brown crushed velvet for the chair, and beige and brown flowered linen for the sofa. I buy the amount of yardage I'm told to get. My grandmother and mother arrive to do the upholstery. After they are done, my grandmother gives me her upholstery needles, so I can try them on my own. "We're going to head out now," my mother says, "so you and Daniel can enjoy the new furniture."

Daniel arrives home and starts petting the cat. He looks over at the sofa expecting it to be seafoam green to match the chair and then looks at the chair to see the seafoam green is gone. He jumps. "I thought you understood," and he looks hurt and leaves.

I call my mother to thank her for the upholstery. I explain Daniel expected the furniture to be seafoam green. My mother laughs. I don't say anymore. She doesn't like to hear bad news.

Daniel decided the bookshelf should be painted green. He dropped me off at the hardware store on East James Street in Kent. "Take care of her," he says to the store clerk. I'm shown to the spray paint aisle. I decide on dark forest green.

This hardware store clerk is a tall man with rectangular shoulders, straight black hair, brown eyes, and almond skin. "Your husband is one of our best customers," the store clerk says as he is ringing up my purchase. "Does he own a construction company?" he asks.

"I don't know what you're talking about," I answer. "My husband never buys things at the hardware store." I'm remembering the time I stopped to buy plumbing supplies when we came back from Des Moines. He didn't even want to be in the parking lot.

"I thought...," he starts to say. "Never mind." My bag of paint is next to his cash register. He notices that it is still there. "Oh wait. I have to give you this." He hesitantly hands me the bag.

Another customer watched our interaction and says to the cashier, "I can't help but notice, if you shared your information and she shared her information, you'd come to a conclusion."

The cashier says, "I have all the information I need."

"Yes," says the customer, "but she has more information." I leave. No one is sharing information with me. I need answers, not questions.

I set up the paint outside, laying down newspapers on the sidewalk. The neighbors compliment my work, the bookshelf is pretty. When Daniel comes home, he complains in a high, stressed voice. "It's the wrong color of green. It should be paler. You made it worse. Can't you do anything right?" He is very upset with me.

Daniel comes home from Seattle Pacific University. I'm sitting in the bedroom. "An Avon Lady moved in next door...," I start to say.

"Oh, this is good. This is good. I'll need to talk to her." He is excited. I hold up the black cherry lipstick and nail polish I bought. Nervously he says, "Put that away. Put that away." He looks in the direction of the other apartment. I put the lipstick in my jewelry box. He kneels next to me by the bed, "I want you to make money for the family. It would be illegal for me to tell you how." He nods at me, smiles, and says, "Do you have it?" I'm expressionless. He leaves and is gone for a full week.

I take a walk down to the pool at the apartment complex. I'm trying to understand this man. "What did he say to you?" asks a woman at the poolside.

"He said he was leaving me alone at night to make extra money, but he couldn't say how, because it would be illegal."

"He wants you to do something illegal instead of him."

"What?" [She understood, but I was still confused.] "He says that I'm dumb." Maybe I am dumb.

"If he wants you to be alone at night to make extra money, then he's the one who is dumb," replies the woman's friend. "Forget about him. I mean completely forget about him."

"I'm thinking of getting a restraining order," I say sadly and weakly, looking down at the patio chair.

"Is he beating you?" the woman asks. Hot tears run down my face as I nod.

"We helped her. Let's go," her friend says. When I looked up, they were gone.

On Wednesday night he comes back. "I thought you had the money for me," Daniel says, appalled. "You mean this whole time you weren't selling Avon. You were buying Avon?"

"It was two for $5 and it was the promotional offer," I defend. To myself I thought, he complains about me spending $5. He spends more than that at the pub.

"I have to get out of here. I'm paying rent to Ross," he says, turning to leave.

"I don't understand why you're doing that. You have a place here," I say, pointing to the bed. He leaves.

He stayed once a week on Thursday night, the other nights he stayed with Ross. We arranged for him to give me a ride home on Fridays after I took the bus to work. This gave him a chance to use my car.

"You don't need to wait for me to give you a ride home. I found someone else to give you a ride. Just wait directly across the street from your work and someone will pick you up."

"You told me never to wait there." This was the parking garage under an apartment complex.

"This time it will be okay. And you should wear this." He holds up an outfit.

I tell him, "No, there are no pockets."

"Pockets, why do you need pockets?" He rolls his eyes and holds up another outfit, "Okay, then this."

"Why am I wearing a certain outfit?" I'm doubtful this would be good for work.

"So, I can tell the driver what you are wearing."

The next morning, I decide the outfit won't be soft enough to snuggle babies at the YWCA Infant Daycare. So, I put on my regular clothes and carry along the shirt he picked out to put over it. I leave my purse and ID at home to keep them safe. I don't know who this person is giving me the ride home. Why is he referred to as the "driver" instead of a "friend"? So I buy a round trip bus pass that morning and keep it with me, just in case. After work, I wait at the designated place. I wait for a long time as car after car goes by. A group of girls come out of the building behind me, laughing, and into the parking garage. I'm looking and quietly waiting. A new white van pulls up. The driver steps out and says, "All in. Yes, you too." He smiles at me. After we are seated, the driver asks, "Everyone has their ID, right?"

"I don't," I pipe up. The driver immediately steps out, the van door opens back up and I'm shuffled out. The girls continue to sit in excited anticipation, clutching their purses in their laps and giggling. If I was expected to pay for the ride, why wasn't I told or asked to get a taxi?

A man and woman come up from behind me as the new white van takes off down the street. "What was that?" the man asks.

"My husband arranged for me to have a ride home," I answered. "Your 'husband,'" he sneers at the word. "Some husband." Defensively I say, "He is my husband!"

"Well, he's not acting like it!" More calmly he asks, "Why were you ejected from the van?"

"I was asked if I had my ID, and I said 'No.'" He shakes his head. "Should I carry my ID?"

The woman answers, "Carry your ID, but don't take rides from strangers."

"Did they look like they were driving you home?" he asks.

"They didn't look like they were from the suburbs. People in the suburbs dress differently." I sadly added, "My husband told me to wear this shirt, but without the shirt underneath."

The man looked me up and down and said, "If you had, you would have been living in it." I don't understand what he means. The man asks the woman, "Did you get the license plate?" She nods.

I would stay and help them with their police report, but the last express bus to Kent will be coming soon. "I need to catch the bus."

The man says, "You need to find out what is happening at your apartment." The statement is confusing, but I dash off. I make it to the bus stop in just enough time to catch the express. I get home and find my husband in our apartment.

He drove from Seattle to Kent without picking me up and after telling me he wouldn't be able to give me a ride home today. His hair is a tousled mess and he is frantic. He isn't relieved or happy to see me. He yells, "Would you start carrying your ID?" He had gotten a call in Seattle and then drove down to Kent. "Is that what you wore?" He rolls his eyes.

"I had to go to work." I would have added the word "first," but it seemed pointless. My day was about going to work, not about the ride home. He is quickly going through our apartment. He spilled coffee grounds on the kitchen floor going through the garbage can. I grab a broom to sweep it up.

As I am sweeping the floor he asks, "Where do you keep the money?"

"You mean like 'under the mattresses'?" This is ridiculous. So this is what was going on in my apartment.

He starts to dart towards the bedroom, and then turns back, "I already checked under the mattress." Daniel told me when we first met, "The best way to hide money is to put it under your mattress. The trick is to spread the money out so that it is flat and mainly at the feet." Was this the reason Thomas lay on the floor for his aching back?

"I don't have any money. You've already taken all my money." I'm exasperated. I worked on the farm growing up and saved what money I was paid. Often, I wasn't paid at all. He never worked and never saved a dime. It doesn't matter how much I give him. It's never enough. He promises to pay me back but never does.

"I have business to settle. You are worth more because you are experienced." He says sarcastically, "Who knew?" I have no idea what he is talking about. Experienced at what? But he seems to question why someone would consider me valuable. "I didn't say you were my wife, a different family member," he says, giving me a tense smile, "to explain the same last name."

"You said I was your aunt!" I exclaim.

"Why would you think it would be my aunt?" he asks. "That wouldn't even explain the last name."

Why did I think aunt? Oh, I know, it is because I'm always financially supporting him. I wonder if I should claim him as a dependent on our income taxes. Would aunt explain the same last name? Who in his family has the same last name? I announce, "Your brother's wife has the same last name."

He shakes his head. "I was expecting you to go along with it," he says. "Now I see this wasn't going to work. I would have to." His sentence trails off. He looks through my jewelry box and finds a folded piece of paper. "What's this? How much is it worth?" he asks.

"It's a dollar. It is worth one dollar," I declare. "Put it back and stop going through my things." The paper is wrapped around a 1927 silver dollar minted in Denver with an imperfection on the face, but I don't tell him that. My grandfather gave it to me. Daniel puts the dollar back in my jewelry box.

"How did you get back home?" he asks.

"I bought a round-trip bus pass," I reply. I'm not so dumb after all. He rolls his eyes. "Well that was a waste of money."

"Apparently not, your 'ride' ejected me from the vehicle."

I go to the dresser and pulled out my ID, partially to make sure it is still there. "Is that where you keep your ID?" he asks.

"My grandmother said to always keep my ID in a safe place." I add, "You know, when your husband arranges a ride for you, it shouldn't be considered as taking a ride from strangers." Daniel has a bewildered look on his face.

My grandfather gave me that dollar and he gave me the car too. Daniel doesn't even use the car to give me a ride home. That night, after Daniel is asleep, I sneak from the bedroom to the living room and quietly remove the spare car key I had let him use. I place the key chain back into his coat pocket and place the spare key on my key chain. Now I won't need to explain why I won't fund his bi-weekly trip to feed the homeless anymore. I thought I was funding a ministry. I'm not interested in a new location on a map. What does he do? He doesn't even make eye contact. I slip back into bed. He didn't stir. The next morning, I give him a ride to Seattle to visit Seattle Pacific University. He hasn't noticed that the key is missing from his key chain.

A stranger comes up to me. "That guy over there says you'll have sex with me if I give him some money. I think it would be fairer if I gave you the money." My husband watched in horror and disbelief as I turned the man down.

"What did he say when you told him we were married?" I ask Daniel. "I didn't tell him." He says the answer as if that was obvious.

"Why didn't you tell him we were married?" I demand.

He's angry with me. "That was a perfectly good John."

"He was going to pay you?" I'm processing this in my brain. I thought it was a test. A man comes up to me asking for sex for money while my husband is watching. It should just be a test that I'd be faithful to him.

He misinterprets my voice tone and assumes I was asking about the amount the John would pay. "It depends on how much he liked it."

I asked the wrong question. "Why did you think I'd have sex for money?" would have been the better question.

My husband had "business to settle." He would have left with my car if I hadn't taken away the spare key. Instead, he stayed behind, "You're going to get what's coming to you," he yells. I ignore him. What game is he playing? I can't keep track. I leave him in Seattle to spend another night alone.

In the background I overhear a conversation, "She had no idea she was supposed to say, 'Yes.' I don't believe he has the relationship with her that he thinks he has."

The John asked his friend, "Is he just going to leave me here with a reluctant worker?" Then the John said, "I can't believe she just said, 'Honey, I got the keys.'"

I calm myself by singing, "One Tin Soldier" as I walk away. Music therapy calms my nerves. A man waiting at the bus stop comments on my beautiful voice. "One Tin Soldier" is a song about treasure, the treasure of peace, and the conflict brought on by greed. My mind was struggling to put pieces together and the song came out.

Monday morning I go into work. My manager is surprised to see me, but pleased. "Your husband left a phone message late Friday that you might be taking a leave of absence. I just checked my phone messages and hadn't called a substitute yet. Now I don't need to."

One of the fathers says, "I saw you standing across the street. I thought about stopping to give you a ride."

"My husband set up for me to have a ride, but it didn't pan out." I'm too embarrassed to explain anymore.

She asks me, "Is your marriage okay?" I explain that I took back my spare car key and left my husband in Seattle. "The weird thing is, he called and said you were taking a leave of absence." After a pause, she calls the police to make a report. She peeks her head out of her office with both hands on the doorframe, "I called the police. They need more information." I'm confused. "Well, I did my part," she says and goes back into her office.

When I get home, I call my husband in Seattle to find out what is up. "I didn't want you to lose your job. You might need something to go back to." I try to get him to explain. He adds, "Right now I'm trying to find a new place to live."

"Aren't you staying with Ross?" That is the phone number I called. I look at the phone to see if it is acting strange.

"I mean a permanent place to live."

"Why can't you live here at the apartment?"

"I planned to cancel the lease. I asked how much notice to give."
"What?"

He yells, "I didn't expect you to take the bus home!" End of call.

At the first of the month, I go to the apartment manager to pay the monthly rent. I always went in person to receive a paper receipt and avoid some weird transfer of funds. They are confused. "Why are you paying the rent? You already paid the first and last month's rent. And this is your last month."

"Last time I checked my name was on the lease," I say.

"Your husband gave notice," the apartment manager informs.

"He didn't tell me," I add quietly. "It was news to me that he moved out. Now that he is gone, I don't need the larger one-bedroom."

"We are out of studio apartments. The rent is about the same now anyway. The rent on studios increased due to demand."

"Do I have to move? I didn't give notice."

"No, you can stay. You already live there and have first right." She gasps, "You used to live in a studio."

"Yes, that's right," I affirm, wondering if she is about to change her mind.

"You're the same one whose husband tried to bury the shovel," she remembers.

"What do you mean, 'bury the shovel'?" I ask. Shovels bury things, you don't bury shovels. The statement makes no sense."

"Well, he tried to make sure it was under things," she informs. I have no idea what she is referring to. We've never had a shovel.

"Okay, if I give notice, it will come from me." I swiftly walk out the door and down the sidewalk. I'm the one who secured the apartment with my savings account. I'm the one who paid the first and last month's rent and deposit. I always pay in person, every month on time. Yet the man who lives there says something and they are all ears. It is a man's world.

"You're talking to yourself," an apartment tenant is on his back porch watching me but smiling.

"Oh, I'm sorry, I didn't realize." I pause and stop.

"I see you walk by sometimes. Usually, your cat is following you." He smiles again because it is funny to see. Then he adds, "I'm practicing my violin and could use an audience. Do you want to listen to me play?"

"Sure." That is certainly better than talking to myself. And I won't need to go back to a lonely apartment. I'm thankful to be reminded that I have a cat. He hands me a cup of coffee, and I sit down on the front porch. He lets me rant about my husband giving notice and not telling me, and then gives me a private concert on his violin.

Later I talk to Daniel on the phone. He says, "I thought you were going to move out instead of explaining what happened." What happened? What happened is that I married a husband who is dumb.
I didn't realize this at the time. He was planning to never see me again, cancel my lease, and keep my car. He had sold me to a group that has girls wait on the street for men in cars. This was the second time he sold me. The first time it wasn't just his mother who sold me, he was in on it.

POISONING RECEIVES HONORABLE MENTION

Poisoning must be the most unreliable form of murder. Either your victim doesn't cooperate or doesn't die. Or the wrong person eats the poisoned food. The first poisoning was his request for me to eat moldy bread, insisting that it would be a form of penicillin. My biology teacher covered this. Penicillin was originally made from cantaloupe mold and is now synthesized. The best mold for penicillin was grown by a woman dubbed "Moldy Mary." Not bread mold, that is just toxic.

The second poisoning was the wedding cake top we finally got back from my grandmother. Wedding cake I didn't get a chance to eat. He told me that we needed to wait until our anniversary day and open it together. And that I would definitely need to eat a piece for both of us because he doesn't like cake. I agreed. Daniel confessed to my parents that he snuck the cake out of the freezer and laced bread mold through it. I made a backup lemon cake just in case the one in the freezer was inedible.

The third poisoning was at VIPS restaurant. I ordered the chili burger. The waitress brought out our food. The chili tasted fine. The burger tasted kind of funny. I ate it anyway. The waitress came up to me nervously and asked what I had ordered. I told her the chili burger. She asked me if it was okay. I said, "Yes." But I was beginning to wonder. The next morning, I was vomiting so badly, there were chili beans flying out of my nose.

"Where are you going?" Daniel asked as I grabbed the car keys.

"I'm heading to the store to buy Liquid Plumber for the sink," I said. "I don't want to leave it backed up like this."

"You feel okay to drive?" he asked.

"Sure, I just won't eat anything else today." I had to skip Easter dinner.

1986

The fourth poisoning attempt was more successful. We had decided how we would handle the holidays that year. We would spend Thanksgiving at my parents' and Christmas at his parents'. All of this was with the façade that our marriage was okay. We plan to head out on Wednesday after work. There was a road advisory due to snow. "What is the advice?" I ask, not sure what a road advisory is.

"The advice is to not drive and to stay home," Daniel explains.

"Oh, we can't do that," I say. "That would mean the only holiday would be with your parents."

"I wouldn't mind that," Daniel says.

"I'll drive," I made it past Olympia through the thickest traffic. The road was covered with snow. Frequent travelers along I-5 created paths that exposed the asphalt below. The overall effect looked like a 1940s pinstriped suit. I hit the ice. I was afraid of crashing head-on. So I turned the car. We ended up backward next to the center divider with a dent above the tire on the rear passenger side. I was shaking. A driver of a passing car stopped to help. Daniel drove the rest of the way to my parents. When we arrived, we had a story to tell. I was shown to my old room. To my disappointment, Daniel had contacted my mother before our arrival requesting separate beds.

On the trip home, Daniel decided we should wait to stop for a restroom and just go straight to the restaurant. We stopped at the Country Cousin in Centralia. The waitress showed us to a table. I moved out of my seat to use the restroom. Daniel looked like he was going to wait there for me. He had a slight look of derision on his face as I stood up to leave. Was he upset I needed to use the restroom? Was he worried I'd be gone too long? I was gone for a very short time. When I came back our table was given to other customers. Daniel was missing. He said he needed to wash his hands and held out his clean hands for me to see. Why would that take so long? "I had to use the bathroom too," he said. The waitress gave us another table. It is nearly two hours before we had a chance to order. I order the vegetable soup like I always do. I ate up the soup but started to feel sick. Daniel verified that I had a fever. He volunteered to drive.

"He said he needed to talk with his girlfriend for a while." The waitress told the manager, "I got the impression he was breaking up with her." I thought he knows we need to get going. I don't know if he said that or not. Why would he refer to me as his girlfriend? Maybe the waitress is confused.

"Was she sick when she came into the restaurant?" the manager asked the waitress.

"No," the waitress answered.

"Then we have another problem." The manager asked, "How old is the soup?"

"I made it today," the waitress said.

"Has anyone else had any?" the manager asked.

The waitress answered, "No."

"Good," the manager said. "Throw out the soup."

We arrived home. My fever was 102F. My fever continued to climb to over 104F. I started to have seizures and convulsions. I was too sick to use the phone. I asked Daniel to contact my college to tell them I wasn't going to make it to class. He didn't call and I had no way to make up the missed work. I got a "C" as my final grade. My work also assumed I was playing hooky. Daniel told me it would be best if I didn't eat or drink anything. I checked my First Aid book. I was to flush with plenty of fluids. I drank tap water while Daniel was at work to avoid dehydration.

I called the Health Department about the restaurant. "Did you go to the doctor?" the health department worker asked.

"How could I get to the doctor?" I asked. "I was too sick to drive."

"Wasn't there someone to take you?" she asked. I mentioned my husband. She started to get suspicious. "Was he with you the whole time you were at the restaurant?" she asked.

I commented, "He was gone for an unusually long time washing his hands. He didn't tell me he was going to be leaving the table. Our table was given to other customers at the restaurant before I got back from the bathroom. And I was really fast."

"Throw out all of your food," she instructed. "I'm serious, Karen. Throw it all out. Clean the entire kitchen and dining room. Buy new food and watch it closely."

When Daniel came home, he was surprised to see me doing better. I explained I was drinking tap water. He looked at the kitchen sink and jumped. He didn't stay for dinner. He said he was getting together with Ross.

The health department called me back. I affirmed he didn't stay to eat. "Now you know," she said.

My college professor encouraged me to contact DAWN and provided the information. DAWN was very concerned that I was getting beatings and he was showing no remorse.

Daniel came to the apartment one Wednesday after work. I thought he was going to stay the night. He said, "No, I'm just going to show you something." He had a bottle of round, green pills, which he was downing with hard alcohol; seafoam green pills and crème de menthe. "Try it." He leaned back against the couch and closed his eyes. I took the bottle of pills into the bathroom and took the pharmaceutical book my grandmother bought for me into the bathroom too. Quietly I turned through the pages. The label on the bottle and the pharmaceutical book showed this was heart medication. I checked the pills and their marking to the pill description. I looked at the patient's name on the label. It belonged to someone else. The patient must have sold his medication to a drug dealer. I quietly left the apartment to talk to a friend I met at the DAWN meeting.

When I came back, my husband was waking up. He looked over at me and asked, "Did you enjoy it?" I smiled weakly and didn't respond much. His behavior worried me. I didn't want to admit that I didn't try it.

Later he called, "I forgot I told Ross I was going to stay the night with you tonight. It was part of our agreement; so that he can spend time with Bonnie." I hear a man's voice in the background. I don't know who the man would be. "Wait, someone just gave me the offer to stay on the couch. Never mind." He hangs up. Ross remembers to spend time with Bonnie, but my husband doesn't remember to spend time with me. But then again, do I really want to spend time with a drug user. I went from being an up- and-coming pastor's wife to the wife of a drug user.

Daniel left the bottle of pills in my bathroom cabinet. "You have the lives of a cat," Daniel says to me and is baffled.

I look up what that means. I explain to Daniel, "According to folklore, the cat comes back after the first eight deaths and stays dead on the ninth death." I would soon regret that comment.

Daniel's parents come to visit. They fly up from southern California. Daniels suggests we pretend our marriage is fine and let them stay at my apartment. I plan the meals and clean. He set up a bed for them on the living room floor by borrowing an air mattress. In the morning, he wants me to wait in the bedroom and allow them to use the bathroom and dress. He doesn't tell me when they are done. I need to use the bathroom, shower, and cook breakfast. At this point, I'm waiting in the bedroom for no reason. I'm furious that he doesn't have the consideration to let me know when I can come out. When I do, I go into the bathroom and throw my brush against the tiled wall, and the brush breaks. Viola calls me a "Wild Thing."

Daniel drives us to church. In church, he is sitting between both of us. I am crying. His mother is crying. He is sympathetic towards his mother. After the service, a woman at the church stops me and says, "Your mother- in-law is fake crying. How could she do that in church?" I pause and look at her, and then join them as they leave. I insist on driving home. It is my car, my apartment, and I'm tired of pretending.

Thomas and Viola are talking quietly in the back seat of my car as I drive them from the church back to my apartment. Thomas whispers to Viola, "She is working and supporting the family."

"Oh, so we aren't treated as the parents of the one who is supporting her," Viola says, putting things together. "Legitimate work?" she asks.

"Yes, legitimate work," replied Thomas. "But he doesn't realize it. We didn't prepare him for this." They quietly gather their things at my apartment.

Daniel offers to give his parents a ride to the airport. "They are my parents." To avoid a conflict, I let him use my car. He is gone for several hours, much longer than needed, eventually, he returns with my car. "I almost forgot I need to return it," he says smiling. The bus system has stopped running for the night. The morning bus schedule will be starting soon. He has a ride back to Seattle. I wonder who would be giving him a ride at this hour? He laughs. "She followed me here in her car." Later he calls, "I don't need to borrow the car this week. I have a car to use."

I try to rephrase what he said, "You are borrowing a friend's car?"

"Something like that," he says. "I just have it for a while, and then I have to ditch it."

"What does 'ditch' mean?" I ask one of the neighbors. "As in ditch a car. Does that mean to park it in the ditch?" The neighbor bursts out laughing. .

Karen Roberts

72

THE LIVES OF A CAT

My husband calls me about a trip to Vancouver BC Expo. I ask, "Will Ross and Bonnie come with us?"

"No just the two of us," he replies.

"Should I put in a reservation for one bed or two?" I ask.

"Just one bed," he replies. Things were looking up. Maybe, just maybe we could reconcile the marriage, or maybe this was the honeymoon period DAWN warned me about. "Be sure to take out enough money for the trip," he adds.

We found a German restaurant at the Expo. I left to use the restroom but kept my eyes on him. As I came to a place where I needed to turn out of sight, I mentioned to another customer, "If I take my eyes off him, something happens to the soup."

"What?" the customer asked.

"Food poisoning," I said.

"I'll keep an eye on him," he agreed and nodded.

"I'll be quick," I promise.

When I came back, the customer informed me, "He stayed put." I walked back to our table with confidence.

I hadn't brought enough money. I hadn't brought money for his alcohol. He insisted on buying beer at the German restaurant. He said he wanted each of us to have one. I hate beer. He forced me to drink some of his beer. I pushed my lips into a tight thin line and put the glass to my lips. The beer foam covered my upper lip. "There," he praised. "That is how I know you've had a good drink when there is foam on your lip." When he turned the other way, I wiped the beer off with a napkin. He didn't notice. None of the beer had gotten into my mouth.

He told me to drive in the left lane to use less gas. He physically beat me while I was driving home on I-5 through downtown Seattle, unlatched my seat belt, periodically pressed his foot down hard over mine on the gas to make the car accelerate and go out of control. In one swift move from unlatching the seat belt, he was grabbing the steering wheel and turning it hard toward the center divider on the freeway. Cars came alongside honking. He was trying to kill me.

I mouthed the words, "Help me!" to the passing cars.

Daniel turned to look at the other drivers watching us and watching my face. "What is it about you that people take one look at your face?" He moves off of me enough for me to steer the car towards the right-hand lane.

"Drive in the left lane!" he yells. He looked to his right and jumped in his seat. We were on a double overpass. It was a long way down.

"No, I'm driving in the right lane and going slow," I assert.

"Slow down," Daniel said quietly. He looked around him. "The other cars are keeping pace with you." The cars were creating a protective buffer on all available sides of my vehicle. "Okay, drive the speed limit." He backed off and stayed in his own seat the rest of the way back.

At DAWN I learned, "A situation looks different from the inside than it does from the outside. That is why it is hard for others to imagine our situation."

When I went to the next DAWN meeting, a group member said, "I want to hear her story."

"I do too," said another. They let me have the floor.

At the end of the meeting, the group facilitators took me aside. "We don't usually do this. We are concerned about your safety. We believe, if you don't divorce and obtain a protection order, you will end up dead." I obtained an Anti-harassment Order and filed for divorce in King County in 1986.

The Avon Lady next door and her new husband were happy that we filed for divorce and happy to see Daniel go. Her husband was happy I make money by doing hard work and already thought that was true.

The man downstairs was happy the loud, banging noise was gone. "No, it wasn't from the bedframe coming apart, the wrong part of the apartment, more in the front." He added, "No, not music," he clarifies, "something else." He assures, "Usually the noise was while you were at work anyway."

The violin player said, "I was wondering when you would be coming back around."

I went from being in the young married group at church to the singles group. I met with Roberta, a former pastor with the United Methodist Church. She was helping with the singles group. She told me about how when she was married, she knew where to go for physical contact. She described how her husband used to massage her feet. "He sounds like a nice man. You must have had a wonderful relationship," I said, wondering why she got divorced.

A woman from the United Methodist church was listening in on our conversation. "How many men did you sleep with when you were married?" she asks me.

I said, "Just one."

Roberta nods. She assumes this is a confession that I slept with one man other than my husband.

The woman from the church lets me know that Roberta continued to misunderstand. I clarify that "just one" means only my husband. I went 1½ years without sex while married; because he wouldn't sleep with me. But I was never unfaithful until we separated. I shrug. Somehow that seemed justified.

Roberta said, "Okay, now I have a better idea of why you got divorced." She didn't know any of it. She never asked me. She talked with someone my ex-husband spoke with and thought she had the whole story. She had the wrong information and she missed obtaining my perspective. The people with DAWN said my ex-husband portrays me as unfaithful to paint me as the bad one in the relationship. It is part of his sickness.

2017

My youngest daughter, CM, was driving my car in Yakima. She was rear- ended while waiting at a stop sign. The driver of the other vehicle called friends at the Yakima County Sheriff's Office, who then called her father and gave him the impression the accident was CM's fault. I called the Yakima police department to set some things straight. A man with a deep voice answered the phone.

"My daughter was in an accident. I checked and the City of Yakima has jurisdiction," I explain. "She was rear-ended while waiting at a stop sign." While I was on the phone, the officer mentions a murder case he was trying to solve.

"I have a case on my desk. There is a man picking up hitchhikers, taking them down a long, lonely road, and then killing them. We think he picks them up to make up for a past wrong and then kills them. I'm searching my database right now."

"You won't find him in your database." I'm certain they have profiled this man incorrectly.

"It's a database of previous offenders," the police officer says. "The person must have a tendency to commit wrong."

"I understand that. But he isn't a previous offender. You said he is picking up hitchhikers, right? He dehumanizes the hitchhiker because he feels it is wrong behavior. He humanizes them by being their savior and giving them a ride. When they feel he is cramping their free spirit and doesn't appreciate him, he dehumanizes them again and this time he kills them. That is what the Green River Killer was doing."

"That is a different motive. The Green River Killer comes to Yakima," the police officer said. "They caught the Green River Killer."

"No, the police officer they suspected didn't do it," I correct him. "They caught another one," the police officer corrects me.

"Another one, and yet, the killings are taking place now in Yakima," I ponder aloud, "Down by EBP Road."

"I didn't say EBP, I said a long lonely road." He asks, "Why are you thinking EBP?"

"My in-laws live near there and it is a long lonely road," I explain. But there are many lonely roads.

"Why did the Green River Killer stop killing in 1984?" the police officer questions. "Did he get better at it?"

I think about the year. "1984 was the year my ex-father-in-law moved from Auburn to California."

"You're wondering if your father-in-law could have done it?" the police officer asks.

I appreciate that he understands. "I know you can tell the height of the killer by the wounds on the victim." Doing the math calculation aloud, "My ex-husband was 5'11" and his father was six inches shorter, so 5'5"."

"I hate to break this to you. But if one of them was the killer; you married him," the police officer said. "What was he doing in January of 1984?"

"He moved to Seattle and lived in an apartment," I answer. "He couldn't borrow his parents' car anymore. He couldn't borrow my car either," I explain. "He had to get around on the bus."

"That would slow him down. How would your ex-husband attack his victim?"

"He is all arms and legs, hitting and kicking," I answer. Quietly I added, "My legs would get bruised up." I wonder if he is going to believe me. Do I have to convince him?

He accepts my answer. "Strikes to the head?" the police officer asks.

"He likes to go after the head," I say remembering back. "He dumped a bowl of pancake batter down onto my head. He hit me with a pillow in the head when I was praying."

"Really, when you were praying?" the police officer finds that curious.

"Yes, it was a decorative pillow and very hard." A K-Mart special that was a splurge at the time when I decided the apartment needed a splash of blue. "His strikes to the head are with an object, not his fists," I repeat back an evaluation from an earlier police report.

"Would he grab a rock and strike someone's head?" the police officer inquires.

"No, he was a baseball pitcher with a dead aim," I answer. "He would take a rock and throw it at the victim's head."

"That explains a lot," the police officer says. "And that is what he would call it? 'Dead aim'?"

"Yes, that is what he called it," I respond. "His baseball coach told him that."

The police officer seems relieved that the conversation wasn't a waste of time. "We are looking for a tall man with a strong pitching arm," he yells to the team.

"It would prevent blood from splattering on the killer," I consider aloud.

"Yes, it would," the police officer agrees. The police officer asked, "Did he ever practice throwing with a rock?"

"No, he'd use a tennis ball and dent the wall in our apartment," I explained.

"How high?" the police officer asks.

"One foot higher than our bookshelf," I say, going into the kitchen to measure. "Six feet high."

"Are you sure?" the police officer asks.

"Yes, I have the 5' bookshelf right here." I'm certain. "It was above by twelve inches."

The police officer calculates. "That is too high for a baseball pitch." Then he adds, "I find it interesting. The location for all of these killings has something to do with you."

"I wouldn't be the right height," I try to get him to understand. I call to report a car accident and now I'm suspected of murder. I say, "I wouldn't do it."

"Yes, I know that." He explains, "But your ex-husband is stalking you. So, the locations have something to do with you."

"I'm not in Yakima right now," I correct him.

The police officer explains, "Yes, but he doesn't know that. Maybe I should put out an APB." I give him Daniel's full name, birth date, and social security number. "I love ex-wives," the officer says. I explain our marriage doesn't immediately come up in the database. "When were you divorced?" I give him the date. "That pops up," he says triumphantly.

"Amazing, so I become a divorcee who was never married," I'm putting this all together.

He chuckles, "Sometimes the divorce decree comes up easier because it is an actual court document."

"I had a protection order too. But it expired. The judge was too soft," I explain. "Too many of her couples died."

"What was the protection order for?" the officer asks. I explain the attack on the freeway driving home. "He wanted you to drink the beer so the TOX report would say you'd been drinking. He was staging it as a DWI." I hadn't thought of him staging it. I thought he was just angry I didn't budget for alcohol.

"Daniel told the judge he wouldn't have been trying to kill me, because he was in the car too," I expand. "He told the judge I was mentally ill."

"And the judge didn't pick up on that?" The police officer observed, "He was wearing a seat belt and you weren't."

"I couldn't fasten the seat belt back up, because I needed my full strength on the steering wheel."

"Yes, I see that. And you were in the driver's seat in the left lane, closest to the center divider. Which means you would have suffered the most injuries." He adds, "I had a feeling you knew something about the case, even before you mentioned your daughter was in an accident. It was something about the way the phone rang." As he is hanging up, I hear him say, "Hey, the woman on the phone thinks her ex-husband might be the killer." I'm about to correct him, but the phone goes dead. I realize he is busy; so, I go back to work.

1985

"Would you please stop doing that? You are putting dents in the wall." I had paid the deposit on this apartment, and I was hoping to get it back. The tennis ball collided with the wall with a loud, bang.

"I need to practice my aim." He continued throwing the tennis ball at nearly the same spot each time.

"Maybe you should join a baseball league." Why doesn't he play baseball?

"Leagues cost money," he argues and continues throwing the ball.

"There is a big field out there. You could throw it into the field," pointing towards the large vacant lot.

"It doesn't work unless it is at the same height," he says but doesn't explain.

"I could stand down there and you could throw it at me," I said, offering to catch the ball.

He misunderstands. "I would never do that to you." He turns towards me and looks me in the face, pleading, eyes wide. "I could never do that to you."

I was about to add "with a mitt," but it seemed pointless.

He turns again and this time he misses, the ball hits the crystal wedding cake top. It shatters and crashes. I scream. He runs out of the room. I pick up the cake top and cradle it in my lap. Tears are streaming down my face. The ring around the top is broken, the symbol of forever. But the blue flower is fine. I could plaster the holes in the wall before I move out. I was overreacting.

He comes back into the apartment, shaking, and says, "Don't ever scream while I'm practicing. I almost … well, just don't ever scream."

"The circle is gone, but the flower is fine," I said trying to make amends. "It was the prettiest part anyway."

"I didn't mean to hit the cake top." He is sorry. "My aim was too low. And it can never be off." He is sorry for missing his target.

My father talked with Daniel on the phone. My father said, "I asked him why he was throwing a tennis ball in the house. Dan said, 'I've been doing that for a while. I never missed it so bad. She must have distracted me.' It didn't make any sense."

I take my car in for an oil change. The oil change attendant says, "You've been getting a lot of miles on your vehicle."

I tell him, "I drive to work in Seattle three days a week, fighting rush- hour traffic, and again on Sunday."

"No, it's more than that," ponders the oil change attendant. He is looking down at the floor and has a frown on his face.

1987

After the Divorce Decree was signed, I went out with friends from the church. I was late then, heading for home. There was road construction on I-5 where several lanes of traffic merge. A maroon van cut in front of a car. The driver of the car slammed on her brake. I stepped on my brake but felt no resistance. My master brake cylinder must be leaking. I should have tapped the brake pedal, but it was too late. I squarely rear-ended the car in front of me. The police came and called for a tow. They spoke with me and the other driver. The driver of the maroon van left the scene. I told the police, "I just want to drive my car to the nearest parking lot and skip the tow. I didn't call for the tow anyway." With some objections from the police, I drove my car to the nearest parking lot, which was the lot for my work. I walked from there. I stopped at McDonalds to use the bathroom. They told me they were closing. With no other options, I finally found a dumpster way out of town and peed there.

The next day, my work supervisor was surprised to see my car in the parking lot but wasn't able to find me. I arrived on time on the bus. So, it was all good. I found a neighbor to help me get it home and my father drove up to show me how to replace the radiator. He replaced the leaking master cylinder.

I receive a call from Daniel about the divorce papers. He waited until the weekend to call. I explain, "That went well, but I got into a traffic accident on the way home. Then I couldn't find a place to use the bathroom. I stopped at McDonalds."

"Why McDonalds?" he asks.

"To use the bathroom," I explain, "Only they were closing and they wouldn't let me. So I ended up going south and peeing by a dumpster. I didn't know what else to do."

"There might be a dead body behind that dumpster," he says. "I went way south," I explain, "Well out of the city."

"Yep, that's the one," he said. "There is a dead body behind it."

"Well, you probably know more than I do." That was all the conversation I needed.

"I was just calling to check if I could borrow the car," Daniel admits. "Now I see that isn't possible."

DAWN said to do the things I've been restricted from doing. I went to McDonalds in Kent. A normal thing most Americans do. I was allowed to take dine in. The McDonalds manager came up to me and says, "I know this may seem like a weird question. But are you the girl who was with the man at the Ronald McDonald playhouse?"

"When they cleared the kids out of the playground?" I ask.

"Yes." He is relieved. "I finally found you. It has been eighteen months, but I never forgot you."

Has it only been eighteen months? It seems like so much longer. Aloud I ask, "Did he hurt the children?" I had to evaluate whether or not to have children with him and that experience weighed in.

"No, we just had to clear them out," the manager explains.

"His parents told me never to take him to McDonalds," I respond. Then I add quietly, with irritation, "even though it was him taking me."

"He acts like he is receiving instructions," the manager gives the reason for the ejection from the restaurant.

"We separated," I inform him, so he won't worry.

"I just wanted to let you know," the manager says gently. As I leave, the assistant manager whispers something in the manager's ear.

The manager asks, "Was it this McDonalds?"

"No, it was the McDonalds in Auburn," I answer. But that wasn't the answer he was expecting. If I read that right, my husband was at a McDonalds in Kent with another woman, while we were married.

"Well, at least one of them came back," he says softly.

I receive a call from Daniel's roommate. "Hey, I'm not sure how you handled your husband. He brought home the swivel rocker and started shredding the upholstery off of the nice chair. I tried to get him to stop. He cut the upholstery off the seat cushion and went berserk. He's just sitting in the chair right now stewing." I can see this in my head. Daniel was removing the brown upholstery to restore the seafoam green. The seat cushion was reupholstered in a different way. The material slips over like a pillowcase and zips shut with an industrial-grade zipper. There was no seafoam green on the seat cushion.

"Look, I divorced him." I proudly assert. "He is your problem now." It took much therapy to not take responsibility for my ex-husband's behavior, behavior I could never control.

The roommate suddenly says, "What? I have to go," and hangs up the phone.

I called later to check on the new roommate, but Daniel said he never had a roommate. I don't know what to think.

A BURIED SHOVEL UNBURIES THE PAST

1987

I decide to add some more paint to the bookshelf. I go back to the hardware store on East James Street to buy the paint. The store clerk doesn't want to sell me any. I look too young to buy paint. I was twenty-one, and because of recent vandalism and graffiti, a new law was passed that you need to be over eighteen to buy spray paint. "Well, I'll take a can of paint and some brushes then." He takes me to the paint aisle and allows me to buy a can of spray paint. I add painter's tape to my basket. I'm going to have fun with this. I select blue paint to accent the green. "I bought this when I was younger and in here with my husband."

I ask about the tall, black-haired cashier who was here before. The manager answers, "He isn't working here anymore after he stopped selling ladders to our best customer." He looks at the man in the back stocking merchandise. "Wasn't it ladders?" the manager asked him. The stocker shook his head no.

I don't have the brain energy to listen to them argue about whether it was ladders or shovels. That's what I'm thinking, isn't it? The manager meant to say shovels. I'm not supposed to stress about the past, just work on moving forward. But, how did Daniel go from not wanting to be in the parking lot of a hardware store to being a customer that encourages them to sell me a can of spray paint? I'm older now than I was then, and I look too young to buy spray paint now.

Daniel lent my jumper cables to a friend at Seattle Pacific University and I needed to drive to Seattle to pick them up. Daniel expected me to tell him to keep them, but I had no intention of doing that. I wanted my jumper cables returned. I didn't agree to have them lent out in the first place. I'm putting the jumper cables in the trunk of my car. I am approached by a man trying to sell me something at SPU. He recognizes me or he recognizes my car, but I don't recognize him. I've never met him before now. He is 5'10" tall, with brown hair and light skin. Daniel would talk of a friend who can't grow a proper mustache but keeps trying, his dyslexic friend who reads everything backward, and the friend who pulled at his hair when he started to go bald and created a pile of hair on his desk. Thomas thought Daniel was going on joy rides with a friend when he borrowed the car. This was probably the friend. The one Dale thought Daniel did marijuana with. He is likely the one who lead Daniel down the wrong path, Daniel's drug dealer, the one who supplied the heart medication, the round green pills he downed with hard alcohol.

"You're the one who convinced my husband to live wild before becoming a minister. You're also planning to become a minister?" I ask. I'll call him Gary, because that is the name I only heard once, and Daniel told me he shouldn't have let it slip.

"Yes, but think of the stories we'll have to tell," Gary boasts with a big smile.

"Why did you encourage him to do drugs?" I interrogate him with a frown.

"Hey, I'm not a bad guy," Gary defended. "This could be something for you too," he encourages with a hopeful look. "You have the money you can live off, don't you?' he prods. "He said he has your parents' money."

"What?" I'm offended. "I'm not interested in this." This is confusing. Why would my ex-husband say he has my parents' money? My parents would never give him money.

"I wasn't counting on this." Gary turned to his friend who returned my jumper cables. His shoulders turned gracefully along with his head, like a salamander on alert. But he turned away from me. He was a bad man, definitely, but not someone I would identify as a killer. "She's going to be a problem." Then he turned to me and warned with a frown, "If you talk about him or me, you will get sued. Do you understand?" His tone was definite and frightening. To his friend he coached, "That is the best way to deal with these types."

I went home and called my parents. "He wants $200," my mother said over the phone. Daniel contacted her for money. He really did. Gary didn't make that up.

"Mom, don't give him any money." My statement is clear.

"Maybe just $50," she said, negotiating down.

"Don't give him ANY money," I plead.

I give the notice to move out of my apartment. I'm moving to a place closer to Seattle to have a shorter commute. The apartment manager tells me Daniel already returned his apartment key. He just mailed it to them. She tells me I need to pay the last month's rent because I had given notice before, but stayed in the apartment. I have them look at the books. I paid by check each month and demanded a receipt too. I paid each rent in person. "You paid the rent that month and we didn't catch it." They both look closely at the record book. "And he didn't tell you he had given notice?"

"No," I softly say and shake my head. How long was he planning my death or disappearance?

"You have a restraining order against him now?" they ask.

"Yes, I have a protection order," I proudly say.

"We should have made a police report," they decide.

"And add that to the other police report," I insert.

"A report for violence." They are angry, "The police should have informed our office."

"No, the report from my work," I corrected. "He also called my work and told them I was taking a leave of absence." They have confused looks at first and then look at each other in realization.

1994

Daniel calls my parents. Later my father tells me, "He was certain he was going to die of lethal injection. We really had to calm him down," my father says. My parents are concerned.

I consider. "Not every state has lethal injection as a death penalty." I'm trying to understand what event started this now.

My father snaps at me, "What does that have to do with anything? Lethal injection, electric chair, he's afraid of all of it!" My father regards me as uncompassionate.

My mother adds, "I asked him if this is because you got remarried last year and he said, 'No.'"

There is a news broadcast on the beatings and deaths of the homeless. For years the police turned a blind eye to their deaths. But there have been too many, especially the rock-throwing. It is becoming disturbingly clear; too many of these deaths were caused by the same man.

2012

I'm seated on the express bus from Portland to Vancouver, coming home from work. A pale woman across the aisle on the bus accuses me, "You claim you were married to him. Judith Mawson says that she was married to him. How do you think that makes his wife feel?"

"I don't know who you're talking about?" I'm thoroughly confused. I don't know these names. "Who are you referring to as 'he' and 'him'?" I ask.

A dark-skinned woman is seated next to me on the bus. She is wearing a flowered dress and a warm full-length winter coat. I'll call her Aurora. She scolds, "Clearly you should stay out of their marriage." The pale woman who made the accusation exits the bus before I have a chance to find out what this is about.

A man on the bus googles the name on his phone and asks me about the Green River Killer. I ask him, "Is it a short man with dark hair?"

"I can't tell," he responds.

I tell him, "The Green River Killer was killing prostitutes and hitchhikers just two miles from my apartment."

The man corrects me, "It was just prostitutes."

I say, "No, I was there. He was killing hitchhikers. I know. I was there. You weren't there. I was there."

The man on the bus says, "I'm trying to rectify this with the previous conversation."

Irritated, I turn to Aurora, "Why did you interrupt?" I ask. "She left. I needed to know why she was talking about the Green River Killer." Aurora closes her eyes and shakes her head; she sits still in her seat, grasping her purse in her lap with both hands.

With a warm smile, the man across from Aurora on the bus asks her, "Are you wishing you didn't get involved in that conversation?"

"Were you married when you lived at the apartment?" the man who was googling asks me.

"No, I had roommates," I answer, "But I was engaged to be married. I had a fiancé." He nods.

Christmas 2018

Daniel contacted my parents to find out what life insurance I have. To my horror, my parents told him the life insurance payouts. They explain this to me at our Christmas party. Their reasoning was so, "He knows what he would be getting." My parents continued to give Daniel $200/month for more than thirty years, totaling more than $70,000. They only now informed me, and they thought I would be pleased. My mother says, "We thought it would be a bonus."

Summer 2019

My parents give Daniel another $1,000 lump sum. They gave him my inheritance as a "program for me." They put him through college, never asking for transcripts to see his grades. My mother wondered why it was taking so long. My father continued to have "unwavering trust" in him and has consistently told Daniel my location since 1986, ignoring the protection order.

With the schooling my parents paid for, Daniel became a counselor. Daniel contacts the state with a file and list of questions to ask me and requests a report of my answers to my psychologist, a report to him. Sometimes it is just one question and the location I mention becomes the location of the next murder victims. The paperwork claims I was found incompetent for making a false complaint. I wasn't, and I didn't. The paperwork says I prefer for the state workers to go to my work or my church. I prefer neither and both locations are harassment. Some state workers ignore the paperwork, noticing that it was submitted anonymously. Others don't notice it is anonymous and do as the paperwork requests.

March 2020

My parents explain at dinner, Daniel told them that when I am found mentally incompetent, he will have me sign over power of attorney to him and he will sell my house and cash in my life insurance. They don't seem to notice any problem with this.

February 2022

Another state worker shows up at my work. I'll call her Amber. She is standing on the manager's side of the desk without a vest. All managers wear vests. "Hasn't it been years since you've gone through menopause?" Amber asks. This isn't an appropriate conversation for the workplace and not a conversation topic we tolerate at Amazon.

"No, it hasn't. It was only last year," I answer, irritated. "I'm only answering because I know you are here to create problems for me. It isn't a topic we tolerate in our workplace and it is a violation of HIPAA laws."

"Right, I'm here to create problems for you," Amber nods. "You're voluntarily discussing the topic."

I respond, "No, I'm really not."

"Does your doctor tell you it is too late for you to be pregnant?" Amber asks.

I answer, "No, as a matter of fact, they don't."

"Is it too late for you to be pregnant?" Amber asks.

"What is this?" I'm about ready to ask for her badge, a visitor's badge, and to check for a tailgate through Security. The state workers used to call me "The Mother of the Messiah." Later they explained they were trying to set me at ease because they thought that is what I called myself. This script is a slight step up from that, but still very annoying.

"You had an administrative hearing in regard to a complaint you made against a professor," Amber declares to justify her reason for being there.

"I didn't make a complaint against a professor," I assert. "The only administrative hearing I had was daycare."

"What was the result of the administrative hearing for daycare?" Amber prods.

"Look, there is no reason to sugarcoat this. You think I had an administrative hearing for incompetency, and I didn't," I assert. "And I didn't make a complaint against a professor."

"If you were to make a complaint against a professor, what would it be about?" Amber asks.

"Look, I'm tired of this rabbit trail. It doesn't produce anything," hoping Amber will stop.

The sort PA tells her, "Karen is writing a book."

Amber asks, "What is your book about?"

I tell her, "It is a trilogy. The first book is about not getting a chance to make my complaint. The second book is about finally making my complaint. And the third book is about wondering why people continue to argue on what my complaint is about."

Amber affirms with satisfaction, "So you admit you made a complaint." I'm taking this comment to mean that she definitely is a state worker. Crissy goes up to her and whispers something in her ear. She turns toward me, "What was your complaint about?" she asks.

"Two murders, you've had the 'who, what, when, where, and why' wrong. Now at least you have the what." Amber stops, slightly. "Did you notice that the file you received showed up anonymously on your desk?" I ask her.

Amber looks worried, "No, I didn't." She knows she is supposed to check.

"It was also flagged by the FBI." I inform her, "One of the many reasons it was flagged is that Viola Bondehagen was mistaken to be my mother by the investigator. Viola claimed to be my mother so that I could be abducted."

"Viola abducted you so that she could be a mother to you," Amber repeats it wrong.

I correct her, "No, she claimed to be a foster mother so that she could sell the girls into prostitution."

"Did you make a report?" Amber asks.

"I make reports, but they tell me they can't find anything illegal." Frustrated I add, "People tell me I frame it wrong." I say more gently, "When you repeated back about Viola, you repeated it wrong."

"I was expecting it to be something pleasant," Amber confesses. "I look to facial expressions to attach meaning." I have no facial expression. I'm simply stoic. She is attaching a facial expression she anticipates, not looking at the one I have. "So, she was luring them into prostitution," Amber reiterates badly.

I correct Amber again, "She didn't lure them into prostitution." This woman has a listening problem. "They were straight-up captured. They needed $10,000 for a down payment on a house in California. She was selling them."

"Selling," Amber says softly. "They had to get $10,000 to buy a house in California. Did any of the girls come back?" she asks.

"There was one," I answer. "I didn't hear much because I was steered out of the room each time an investigation was done."

"You might be the only one who knows," Amber says. "What do you remember?" she prods. "Were there any girls missing, any at all?" she asks.

"Of course, there were," I answer matter-of-factly.

"What do you mean, 'Of course there were'?" Amber hesitantly asks.

"The Green River Killer was active in that area at the time and dumping bodies just two miles from their house." I won't sugarcoat that either. "The only thing is, they caught the Green River Killer and he confessed. But he confessed to killing about ninety girls and they only found forty-nine bodies. It is a small problem, but only a small problem." I stop to consider. "Much better motive, the guy they caught was just a John. The file that showed up on your desk was anonymous. You know what you are supposed to do with that," I remind her.

"Yes, I do know what I'm supposed to do with that," Amber agrees with a smirk.

"Viola Bondehagen was assumed to be my mother in the file, instead of my mother-in-law. The FBI got that right when they flagged it," I explain. But Shannon, an IT Specialist, resurrected the file and removed the mention of the flag."

I called the FBI to enforce this when it happened, but I got no response. The Hillsboro Police Department regarded it as a "minor inconvenience" and the Ridgefield Police Department merely minimized the problem with, "Sometimes that happens."

"Of course," Amber says. "Why resurrect a file and leave in the mention of the flag?" She seemed to be getting it but was only mocking. "You know, the FBI may not have known all the reasons the file needed to be flagged." She considers. "If it was a true story, you would make a report to the police."

"What do you think I've been doing?" I'm getting angry. "Then I get this, 'So you admit you made a complaint,'" throwing her words back at her.

"You said Viola was your mother-in-law." Amber asks, "Who were you married to?"

"Dan Bondehagen," I say. Is she finally paying attention? Does she assume I was talking about a professor? These state workers endlessly assume I'm talking about a professor.

Amber says to the sort PA, "This isn't the type of mistake we like to make," as she turns to leave.

The file can't be closed; because it was never a legitimate file in the first place. It continues to circulate with nothing to stop it. It circulates at my work, my church, my graduate school. It prevented me from obtaining my teaching certificate. It prevented me from many things. There are too many things wrong with the file to explain.

Flashing back to 1985

I'm talking with Daniel at the apartment about the time the man in the old white Toyota sedan picked me up to give me a ride, and I was so frightened. "I think he might be the Green River Killer," I confess. I had wanted to say that for a long time. I choke back tears and hide my face in my hands. The back of my throat is dry and sore.

"How did you know the Green River Killer was picking up hitchhikers?" Daniel asks.

"That's what I was told," I confirm. I hadn't seen the news. I only knew what Amina's friend had told me.

"Why do you want to talk about him so much?" yells Daniel.

"He was killing girls just two miles from your house," I tell him. Certainly, he would find this alarming.

Daniel looks up and thinks about it, eyes moving right and left as if he is adding numbers in his head. "Really closer to seven miles." He looks back down at me and smiles.

"I was all through there," I tell him. "It was a walkable distance. The first kill was a walkable distance. Look I'll calculate the hypotenuse." I grab

95

the calculator/ "The square root of two squared plus 0.7 squared." The answer is slightly more than two and less than three miles. I hold up the calculator for him to see.

He doesn't look at the calculator. He darts out of the apartment. He is gone all day and it is getting dark. I don't leave the apartment, because I need to know when he returns my car.

I step out onto the balcony of the apartment complex. The sky is dark with stars. The frogs are making chirping noises in the marsh across the street. The air is still and cool. It is peaceful and calm. I breathe it in. My neighbor comes out onto the balcony. "I overheard your argument," he admits. "What was your husband doing on the nights the killings took place?" I softly laugh and shake my head. "You think I'm joking, but I'm not. Was he gone those nights?"

"He is always gone." Even now he was gone again.

"Doing what?" he asks.

"I don't know," I admit, wondering.

"Think about that," he says and he goes back inside. The night is less peaceful and now lonely. I really don't know where my husband is. The night is starting to get cold. I turn to go back inside my apartment.

Daniel is gone all through the night and into the next day, twenty-three hours. When he comes back home, he is smiling and relieved. "I took care of it," he says.

"I missed church." He finally brought back my car. "I stayed home and read." I read the Bible and pretended I was in church.

"I need to get some sleep," he said, heading for the bed. He was awake through the night.

"I'll go to the store for milk." I walk to the store, partially to give him a chance to sleep and partially because I'm done being cooped up in the apartment. I return with the milk and he is still awake.

"I saw you didn't take the car," he noted. "Good thing. I forgot to clean out the trunk."

Later the next-door neighbor tells me, "I'm moving to a different apartment. I wish you luck."

I go back inside and see my husband awake, "I wonder if we are going to get new neighbors. Our neighbors are moving away." I see Dan has an intent look on his face. "What?" I ask. I'm worried about the neighbor's safety.

"What did he say to you?" he asks.

"He said he was moving," and that's all he needed to know.

The next morning, I go out to my car to go to work. The apartment managers are there to talk to me, "Some of the tenants saw your husband cleaning out the trunk of your car and throwing things into the dumpster. We can't have this. What was he doing?" they ask.

"I don't know. I'll talk to him." I ask, "Is there a limit on how much we are allowed to put into the dumpster?" I'm trying to clarify the problem.

"Actually, no," they reluctantly admit. "It's just that someone saw him throw away a new shovel."

I don't know if he really threw away a shovel or not. We don't have any need for a shovel. When I get home I told him, "They admitted there is no limit on how much we're allowed to throw away in the dumpster. But let's just throw away trash bags for a while."

He smiled, "I'm glad I let you handle that."

"The car was low on gas." I had to stop for gas on the way to work. I always fill the car up on Friday after work to avoid an extra rush on Monday mornings.

"Really?" he says. "I filled it up twice." So, he burned through three tanks of gas. At what speed, I wonder. He attempts to console me. "The other tenant decided he was just letting his mind run away with him." He tries to get my attention. "Did you hear me? He decided he was just imagining things."

"So did you throw away a new shovel, or not?" I ask. I hadn't asked before.

"Why do you keep going on about a shovel?" He is angry and doesn't answer my question, and this is the first time I've brought it up. I had always read anger to mean my information is wrong. Now I'm not so sure, maybe I'm reading it backward. I need to pay more attention. Treat it like an experiment and figure out when a person is lying and when a person is telling the truth.

August 1984

I locate the number of the group health 24 hour nurse, dial the phone, and, after a brief wait, I explain my symptoms, "The vomit comes out of my mouth with so much force it sprays the back of the sink."

The nurse responds, "They call that projectile vomiting. Your body is trying to rid it itself of something. Let your body do what it needs to do. Does that help?"

"Yes," I answer, feeling relieved.

"And drink water," the nurse adds. She asks more questions about my symptoms.

The nurse calls later to check up on me. I inform her, "I'm doing better. I'm making it to the toilet before I vomit. The vomit is now water instead of yellow stuff. My husband decided he must have gotten me sick."

"The yellow fluid is bile. Your liver was breaking down." After a pause, the nurse adds, "I've checked. The only thing that can break down the liver is in something dead. It can't survive in something alive."

"Well, I'm doing better now," I answer.

"Your husband must have gotten it too. He just didn't show it the same way. One last question," the nurse asks, "does your husband work at a morgue?"

"No, he doesn't," I admit. I'm glad that is the last question.

The nurse mumbles softly, "That was going to be my last question. It would explain…" She doesn't finish the sentence.

I interrupt with, "Thank you for your help." I'm happy not to answer more questions. I married a theology student, not a mortician.

February 2022

I missed two therapy appointments in one day. One appointment was for Dealing with Fears & Anxiety, and the other appointment was for Dealing with Stress. I was charged $80 for missed appointments. I've been too consumed with writing all this down. I decided I'd better send off what I've written so far to CM so she can proofread it for me and plan what to do. I send off an email with an attachment; which I know she will ignore. So, I also send a text message.

Text messages with her reply:

What book?

You said we were writing a trilogy, three novels each novel has a prequel. A trilogy about what? I have no idea what you are talking about.

Maybe you weren't serious. I thought you were.

Are you sure this was a conversation you had with me? Not someone else?

Yes, with you. You are the most talented writer I know.

When was this conversation?

A while back, I don't get to talk with you very much.

How long is "a while"? Weeks? Months? Years?

Less than a year ago.

And you are sure it was with me?

Yes, I don't talk with any other writers; and I don't take out loans for their college education.

The problem is if I am wrong about that, what else am I wrong about? I don't really want to believe my ex-husband was the Green River Killer. I was always sure the killer was the man in the old white Toyota sedan. Even if my ex-husband didn't kill the forty-nine girls, and just buried one in 1984 and killed two in 2017. I don't want to think that is a possibility. I'd rather believe I was mentally ill. But that is the same way I felt when I was solving the murder case. I'd rather be wrong. So maybe I'm not. I need to find someone who will give me an idea of what records to search for. I'm pretty sure if my ex-husband killed anyone, it was throwing a fast pitch to the head. It would have to be an area he was in at the time; although, he may have moved the body. No one hitches a ride down EBP Road. It was the location I named when I was asked about the loneliest road. One of those obnoxious questions I'm expected to answer to a state worker who "reports back to my psychologist." Even though I have no psychologist and I keep telling them that.

And meanwhile, I not only have to deal with this circulating file. I have to deal with my neighbors being told to report where it is I work, where I go to church, and the license plate number of anyone who visits my house. Continued visits from state workers who are instructed to report back my answers; not realizing they are helping someone I have a protection order against. I had wanted a partner in solving this one. This case is more personal and harder to solve.

Flashing back to 1985

"I can't see horror movies anymore," I complain to Daniel. "That was so scary. They couldn't catch him because he changed his MO."

"What is MO?" he asks.

"I'll look it up." I grab the dictionary off the shelf. "You always make fun of me for looking up words in the dictionary."

"It isn't a word," he corrects me to show he is smarter. "It is an acronym."

"It will still be in here. Just you see. Here it is." I silently read through the list, **1** mail order **2** medical officer **3** Missouri **4** modus operandi **5** money order. "Modus operandi," I declare aloud. "I'll look it

up in Foreign Words and Phrases. Not there."

"That means the phrase is Latin," I continue. Daniel scoffs.

I wasn't done yet. "Modus operandi means a mode of operation," I said in triumph.

"What does that mean?" he asks, acting like I didn't answer the question.

I translate it from Latin and he wants to know what it means. Why doesn't he think of me as smart? "Mode of operation means he changed the way he does things. He changed the way he commits the murder. Oh, look, '**Moabite** *n* a member of an ancient sematic people related to the Hebrews, from 'Moab ancient kingdom in Syria.' I didn't know Moab was in Syria. Ruth was a Moabite. That means she was a Syrian woman." He looks down at me in derision and leaves. "I wasn't saying that I was a Syrian woman," I say loudly to him as he is heading out the door. Just when I thought we had a conversation to talk about.

Later I discuss that conversation with a friend. "I don't know why the conversation bothers me so badly."

"Maybe you don't want him to think of you as a Syrian woman," she says. No, that's not it.

2012

He was getting ideas on how to kill these people from me? I wonder.

"How is he getting ideas from your head? Is he siphoning them out with a straw?" jokes the investigator.

"No." I laugh. He is finding a nice way to tell me I'm wrong. I appreciate that. "It's hard to explain."

"I believe you're wrong about that," the investigator says gently. "But I think you are right about these other things. You can smell a murderer. There is something about your past that makes you spot them right away. Think about that." I sensed that he was right, but the difficult thing has been finding which memories to pull.

1985

We head out to a large, open field, halfway down the road. "I saw this place and thought it would be perfect," he says.

"For what? What are we doing?" I ask.

"You'll see," he says. He unveils a wide, blue plastic bat and a white plastic ball with holes on one side. He must have picked this up at K-Mart in the toy section.

"It is a whiffle ball," he says. "It has holes on one side to catch the wind. So it is impossible to throw it straight," he says, smiling. "People usually play catch with it for fun." He hands me the bat and goes a long distance out to throw the ball.

"I don't think the pitcher needs to be that far back," I shout. He throws the ball and it goes wide. "I'm a good batter, but I'm not that good." He is disappointed. I assume he is disappointed with me.

He reluctantly admits, "You're right. I need to be closer." He steps closer and throws the ball again. This time I can hit it. The ball goes far into left field, near the muddy part. I thought he would be angry, but he is excited. "I'll get it." He runs and grabs the ball to throw it again. We practice for a couple of hours.

"Could we play catch with it?" I hadn't had a chance to throw it too.

He firmly shakes his head. "No." We silently walk back to the apartment.

I talk to my mother on the phone and tell her, "And we went to a park to play whiffle ball. It was so much fun."

Later, on another day, "We could play whiffle ball again," I said hopefully.

"No, it doesn't work. It comes in too low. I don't have time to pick up the second one," he says.

"Did you buy another whiffle ball?" I thought we only had one. He was insistent I never lose it.

"No, no other whiffle ball," he says and is angry I'm pressing the subject.

Flashing back to 1986

I find the whiffle ball in the living room of my apartment while I'm cleaning. It is dirty and the plastic is rough and peeling. It is no longer smooth. I'm sitting on the love seat, holding the whiffle ball in my hand. Dan comes in the door. "What are you doing with that?" he asks.

"I never had a chance to throw it," I say. All this time, I never had a chance to play catch with it.

"It doesn't work," he says. "Put it away."

"Should I throw it away?" I ask, wondering why it is so worn.

"No, I might need to use it again." He says angrily, "Just put it away or I'll throw it at you."

Later I talk with one of the neighbors. "Now you know what he is doing with his time," she says. "He is having an affair, and they are playing whiffle ball."

"If they were playing catch with it, the ball wouldn't be so worn." I look at her friend for suggestions. He tells me they need to go. They turn and walk off. I go back upstairs to my apartment.

"You don't need to pay the rent this month. I already have that arranged," he says. He tells this to me on a Friday. I already paid the rent on Wednesday. He has no financial sense. I just smile and nod.

On Sunday morning, "What do you want for your last meal?" Daniel asks as I'm standing in the kitchen. Then he laughs. "Get it, last meal."

I never really understand his jokes. "The only thing I can think of is the same thing Jesus ate at the last meal, unleavened bread and a goblet of grape wine." I'm planning a Sunday school lesson for the kindergarten class and trying to decide what activity to do. Then I gasp, "I could make unleavened bread with the electric skillet. That would be perfect. Thanks for the idea." I search for the recipe in my small wooden recipe box.

"This never works on you," he says disappointed. "That is Last Supper, not last meal," he corrects.

"Is it Last Supper?" I'm very confused and can't remember. "Oh, you're right," I agree. "It's a good thing you caught that," I praise. "I'm glad you corrected me before I taught the class. I always get 'Good Friday' and 'Black Friday' mixed up too." I shrug my shoulders. I look at him, but his facial expression seems wrong. Then I add, "Well it probably was his last meal too; unless they fed him in prison before beating him." *Fed him before beating him,* something about the phrase is stirring to me.

"That's not what 'last meal' means," he says.

"What does it mean? I'd look up the phrase in the dictionary, but I don't have time and the phrase might not be there." He walks out of the apartment and goes to wait in the car. I decided to check the dictionary anyway. No "last meal," just "**last minute** *n*: the moment just before some climactic, decisive, or disastrous event."

"Let's spend the day in Seattle after church," Daniel says when I get out to the car. I have my electric skillet and grocery bag in hand. I put the items in the back seat.

"We can drink the grape juice while we are there," I decide, trying to accommodate the "Refrigerate After Opening" instructions on the Welch's container without an icebox.

Daniel shakes his head in derision. "Let's go to someplace nice."

"Like we did when we were first married," I say with a smile. "Did you bring the whiffle ball?" I ask. Maybe we would finally have a chance to play catch.

Daniel leans his head out the window with a wide smile and says, "I have everything I need."

It is amazing how long it has been since we'd gone out. We park the car in the garage across from the church. After Sunday School and church, I put the electric skillet and remaining groceries in the trunk. We walk down to the pier.

"Have you ever taken the trolley?" he asks. All this time I've been in Seattle, I had never paid any attention to the trolley. We hop on at the end of the pier and get on and off as we visit the different shops along Puget Sound. The sky is clear with a slight breeze. We plan to go to the aquarium, but it is closed for tank cleaning. We stop to eat at a diner that has a toy train. The train travels along the tracks and stops at your table with your food order balanced on top. Fries and a burger served in style. But the diner is closed down. "I can't believe it!" Daniel exclaims. He clearly wanted the day to be perfect. We read the sign from the Health Department.

"The food was never that good anyway," says the man walking by. "When they could no longer serve food on the train, people stopped coming."

Instead, we go to Ivan's Fish Bar for fish and chips. We take a table outdoors and the birds wander at our feet hoping for a crumb of food. Then we stand at the pier and watch the sunset over the water. The clouds in the sky weren't fluffy; they looked thin, delicate, and fragile, like china plates turned on their sides, and starting to take on the shade of the orange-pink sunset. "I'm going to let you help me feed the homeless," Daniel says. The robin's egg blue sky slowly became darker. "It's time," he says. I point to the sign for the soup kitchen. "No, not there," he says, shaking his head. We walk closer to the train station to a bad part of the city. Daniel has been coming here once every two weeks to feed the homeless, always on a Sunday evening. The lights behind blackened windows created a gray tone to the street. But there was no trash. The sidewalks were clean and swept. "They work hard on that," Daniel responded to my survey of the sidewalk. The air was stagnant as if the wind forgot how to breathe. "This area is protected from the wind off the Puget Sound by those buildings." He points toward the east.

I'm stopped by a homeless man. "I need money for a pay phone," he says. A pay phone call is 25 cents, so I give him a quarter. "I need more than that," he says. "I need to call President Ronald Reagan at the White House to make a complaint." I take a closer look at this man. He is unsteady and smells strongly of hard alcohol.

"You're going to use the money to buy alcohol," I accuse.

"What if I am?" he retorts.

Daniel intercepts, "I'll take care of him later."

One of the other homeless men is concerned and asks me, "Hey, what did he mean by I'll take care of him later?"

I respond, "Don't you recognize him?" Daniel has been feeding the homeless here every two weeks for nearly two years. Certainly, some of the homeless people would recognize him as a friendly, helpful face.

The man who asked for change straightens up. "I'm sober now," he says in a fearful tone to the one who asked what Daniel meant. As we walked past the soup kitchen and I saw their reaction I realized, I didn't look up the wrong phrase in the dictionary this morning. I looked up the right one. Daniel never fed these people. All this time I was allowing him to use my car and giving him money for two meals. He was only spending the money on himself.

Daniel steers me away from them, "I don't want them to recognize me," he says as if that is obvious. "As a special treat, I was going to let you throw."

"Throw?" I ask.

"I would throw too," he says. "There can be no misses."

"Is she watching him?" one of the homeless asks another.

Another answers, "She's watching him and she's watching us." I'm looking at their reactions.

Daniel looks down at the far corner of the park, "There used to be a pile of rocks here," he says inspecting the ground. "They cleaned it up."

"Part of the beautification project?" I ask.

"No, something else," he says. "I'm going to need to find a new location. I'll look at a map."

He looks at my uncomprehending expression. "I thought you wanted to—never mind. Let's go home." He quickly starts to walk back. "Usually, I'm able to move through anonymously. I can't do that with you," he complains.

"Do you mean throw at the park?" I ask. It is getting dark and the park has no street lights. "We are passing the park." I'm trying to get him to stop and then I'm running up to be alongside his fast stride.

"She is trying to get him to play catch." One of the homeless men warns me, "Lady, you need to be careful around that guy."

"He is my husband," I call back. The homeless man steps back. I came here to help the homeless. Instead, they helped me. They were like birds in the forest who warn animals of an incoming predator. I'm forever grateful to them. I couldn't help but smile at them.

"Don't smile and wave at them!" Daniel shakes his head. "My God, you are just stupid." Daniel is silent all the way home and disappointed.

February 2022

I'm reading and I find this news article, "Patches the Clown" was the character played by John Wayne Gacy, a child party entertainer who became a serial killer from 1972 to 1978. He had thirty-three kills, mostly young boys. At the time, I had no idea what Daniel and his parents were talking about. Daniel was obsessed with Patches. He saw his face everywhere and would go into an angry stew each time.

I read back over what I've written so far. I decide that now might be a good time to hire a private detective. My daughter and I have tried this before, several times, but it didn't work. I find a 2020 copy of the yellow pages, the last year it was delivered, and dial for Clark County Investigations. A man with a gravelly voice answers the phone, "Investigations."

"What type of investigations do you do?" I ask.

"First, tell me about your case," he inquires.

"Well, it's hard to know where to start. It is a long story and it is hard to shorten it," I start to answer. I don't really like discussing my case over the phone. Rapidly I say, "My neighbors have been asked to watch my house and report the license plate of anyone who comes to visit. That is the most immediate concern. I had a protection order against my ex- husband, but unfortunately, it expired. He has an APB out on him from the City of Yakima in connection with murders that were happening on EBP Road in Yakima. There have been people visiting my church and workplace with a file that claims my doctor involved them—"

The detective cuts me off. "I think I've heard enough of your case. We aren't a government agency. We're private. We do criminal investigations here, criminal cases, corporate. We don't do domestics. You can contact law enforcement. They work for you for free."

"I've tried that," I respond, "several times."

"Any detective agency charges $250/hour with a ten-hour minimum," he says. "That means you are looking at paying $2,500. Does that put it into perspective for you?"

"You're talking to me as if I don't know things," I say.

"I was trying to let you down easy," he admits. "Apparently, that didn't work." More strongly he asserts, "I'm not taking your case." He hangs up.

Work is finally slow. I have the day off. The building my daughter works in is shut down for a long weekend for repair and maintenance, so she has the day off too. This doesn't usually happen. I book a hotel close to the Capitol Building and we travel to Olympia to visit family. We hike to the Capital building, enjoy the water fountains, look at the monuments, and see the boats along the marina.

My aunt and uncle invited us to dinner at a nice restaurant. I discuss the book I am writing and my uncle is skeptical. "Who was murdered?" he asks sarcastically.

I remember the list, forty-nine victims including two unidentified, "I could print you a list of forty-seven names," I explain, "I'm not angry with you. I'm angry with the Attorney General's Office for using FBI flagged files and leading people down the wrong path. The attorney generals are going to fry. One of the reasons for the FBI flag is Viola Bondehagen pretending to be my foster mother instead of my mother-in-law."

"You can't take on the Attorney General's Office," my uncle says.

"I can. I will. And I'll win," I assert.

This is lunchtime during a weekday, less than a mile from the capitol building. Two men at the restaurant overhear the conversation I'm having with my uncle and start up their own conversation. "Usually, the FBI flags a file because the case was expunged. I think of a flagged file as something I can use," the state attorney admits.

His dinner guest responds, "You are assuming you know the reason the file was flagged."

The state attorney explains, "I didn't think of it as something that would lead me down the wrong path and keep me from doing my investigation."

Later I discuss the conversation we had at lunch. "At least he finally asked the right question, even though it was sarcastic."

"In a way, 'Who was murdered?' is still the wrong question," my daughter responds. "It would seem obvious from the conversation that your ex-husband committed murder. I wonder why he didn't think of it."

"He's met my ex-husband," I reply. "He doesn't want to think that way about someone he has met."

"What does he look like?" she asks.

"He is tall with balding hair and blue eyes," I answer. This vague description is enough. The only men who come to the house are two short, Hispanic men who do lawn maintenance and tree trimming.

"I'm going to warn the neighbors," she responds. Alert the neighborhood watch. She has the best ideas.

February 24, 2022

I'm coming out of work. I take off my work vest, put on my coat and zip it up, take down my hair, and take off my face mask. In the parking lot, I stop to view the layer of snow on the ground that softly blows up off the road and finds a new place to settle. It is going to be a slow and difficult drive home. I search for my car keys in my clear bag and put them ready in hand. One of the packers stops and asks about my book. I tell him I need to get busy writing.

A sorter from work tells me, "There is a different presence about you."

"Oh." I didn't realize a problem. I nod. "To write the book, I need to get into my ex-husband's head."

"What is your book about?" a woman asks. I'll call her Athena.

"My memoirs," I say and wink. "That sounds boring enough."

Athena standing near the door starts to mock me. Or she didn't. For some reason, I block these things out of my head when they happen. Someone is harassing me and I'm not sure who is behind it. It is too overwhelming, too frightening. It is a dissociative reaction and it doesn't help me. The protection order does nothing. Something in the back of my head says, "No." So I'm not sure later if it happened or not, even though it was just yesterday until someone brings it up again. Mocking is about them, not about me. I shake it off. If I remember right, and I don't really want to remember, the conversation went like this. "You're trying to make money off of a murder," Athena accuses.

I respond, "You haven't read the book. That's not what the book is about."

"You can't prove any of it," Athena claims.

"Yes, I can prove it. How many people are able to throw a baseball at 100 mph? How many can you count? Don't bother to think of percentages, what is the actual number? How many can throw a rock at that speed? A baseball, a softball, a tennis ball are all aerodynamic and have a low moment of inertia. A rock is uneven. The moment of inertia is higher. How many can throw a rock at killer speed with dead accuracy? How many pitchers practice their throw and put dents in the wall? Of those people, how many would do it? You'd be surprised what I can prove," I defend.

It's similar to the ambidextrous killer in my second book. The autopsy report stated, "No right- or left-hand preference." For many years law enforcement took the statement to mean there was no way to narrow it down. But the reverse was true. The knife strokes on the body would be difficult to do without showing a preference. Not many could be that ambidextrous and have a predisposition to commit wrong. Only one was in the house with the victim. And in this case, too, only one person could and would make the throw.

"If that's true he could move on from attacking the homeless to attacking other people," Athena mocks.

"I'd say he is a stone throw away from doing that," I retort.

The sorter questions Athena, "Why are you coming after her instead of the killer?"

Athena is stunned. "I assumed they already investigated him."

"You do this every time. You first hear of it and assume it is already investigated," I accuse.

Security is right inside, and another worker runs in to get her. Security is more riled than I've ever seen her. "We've been looking into this. Most of these visits aren't legitimate. You aren't allowed to go to a person's work."

Athena explains to Security, "I was following a script." A script again, but the script has been changed. It is no longer a script about trying to make me believe I'm pregnant and then a second script trying to evaluate my mental competency for thinking I might be pregnant after menopause. The script now focuses on trying to keep me from writing this book.

"And who gave you that script?" Security asks. "Who is the only person who could have given you that script?" Athena stands silent.

"This is a total creep," another worker says, "That idiot woman didn't consider who had given it to her."

"There is an APB out on my ex-husband," I say. "I've submitted information about him, but someone keeps deleting it from the database."

Security nods. "We found out who was doing that too," Security proudly responds. There is no more need for me here. I turn to walk away and plan for the icy drive home.

Behind me, I overhear a conversation. "Don't call the police," I hear Athena cry. "I'll lose my license."

"You'll lose more than that!" Security tells her. "You're not going to see your family again. You're not just going to jail; you're going to prison."

I manage the drive home, pulling off the freeway a few times, and stopping at Starbucks for coffee. The usual forty-five-minute drive takes five hours. But it was successful. I can't complain. On an earlier trip home after work in a blizzard, I stopped at McDonalds. They weren't open yet. So, I slept in the car, waiting for 6:00 a.m. When I went in, I ordered breakfast; folded egg, coffee, and orange juice. I sat down and intently watched the weather with dread. I-84 was closed due to the blizzard at Hood River. The remaining drive home would be difficult. I clutched my coffee in my hands to warm them up. A woman came up to the cashier, "That woman was sleeping in her car," she reported. "Aren't you going to do something about it?"

The cashier replies, "You're supposed to pull over and sleep if you're tired. Not everyone works dayshift. Some people work nights. She drove a long way here and has further to go." I hadn't said anything to her. They saw on the camera what time my car pulled into the parking lot. They saw my employee badge. They saw the emblem on my work jacket. They knew I had driven up from Oregon. I had ordered a large breakfast and sat down to eat. So this was the end of my workday, not the start. And they saw my expression as I watched the weather, so they knew I had farther to go. Even though years ago, I was ejected from the restaurant with two "to go" bags, I have to hand it to these people.

1983

Daniel is sitting in the living room at my apartment in Auburn facing the picture window. He is wearing gray jeans and a purple plaid shirt. "Do you have a best friend?" Daniel asks.

"Yes, my best friend is Christine. She went to Pacific Lutheran University to become a teacher. PLU didn't have the program I wanted, so I came to Green River," I answer. I look at him, expecting a pleasing response, as I walk from the sofa to the kitchen to get him something to drink.

Daniel rolls his eyes. I'm boring him. I stop in the living room and listen. "I made a pact with my friend," Daniel brags. He leans back in his chair. "The biblical kind. And we did it up right." [Ref 1] "We put a lot of thought into whether girls should be treated as birds and decided they should be," he stops to consider and remember the debate. "I wasn't sure, but he insisted they must," he says. "This is our time to have fun. We made a pact that whoever is caught first takes the rap for the whole thing." He frowns and looks down. "I can't really do that to him, but he said he'd be okay."

I think about running to get my Bible to look up the passage he just mentioned. My legs start to move into a sprint and then freeze still instead. My upper body remained motionless. My knees merely wobbled to the right. I think about what he just said about his friend. "I would never let my friend take the rap for something," I assert. How could I do that to Christine?

"He said he'd be okay," Daniel defends with a frown. Then he looks up at me and smiles. He misunderstands my assertion, but he doesn't realize it. He thinks I won't let him take the rap for something he has done. I don't realize the misunderstanding either. I was saying I wouldn't let Christine take the rap for something I had done. We talk in two different languages.

[Refl. Daniel is referring to The Book of Genesis 15:9–18 where Abraham brings a heifer, a goat, and a ram, along with a dove and a young pigeon to God. The animals, except for the birds, are cut in half and God walks through the pieces to make it clear that if the covenant is broken this will happen to him and worse. If you read it carefully, it is only God who walks through the pieces, not Abraham.]

January 1994

The care of an elderly woman in Magnolia didn't pan out after nine days of work with no day off. I moved in with Daniel in his apartment in Seattle. I already paid his rent for him anyway. It was a dark, dingy place in the basement of a two-story house, but Daniel loved the location. We slept separately on twin bunk beds.

Daniel's friend in Seattle couldn't use his truck anymore and got rid of it. Thomas wouldn't let Daniel borrow his car, insisting he could take public transportation. I followed Thomas's line of thought and refused to lend my car. It was a good opportunity for Daniel to buy a bus pass and learn the routes. Daniel talked to his friend. "He is disappointed, but he says it can wait another month."

Daniel got his aggression out by taking my Christmas presents that I had gotten from my family and throwing them long and hard against the asphalt on the road outside the apartment, smashing each one, and seeing them shatter. The neighbors came to the door to complain, concerned that someone might become injured. I complained to them that those were my Christmas presents. Obviously, I couldn't stop him.

"If it happens again, we'll call the police," the neighbors warn.

I peek my head out the door and quietly whisper, "Please do." Then look behind my shoulder to see if he saw me. He was in the other room.

February 1994

I was practicing taking vitals for a class to prepare for the practical exam. Daniel mocked me for taking the pulse at the wrist. "That is how you tell," he said as he pushed his index and middle fingers hard against my left jugular vein. He pushed so hard I couldn't speak.

When he let go, I stifled a scream. "Doesn't that hurt the patient?" I asked after he let go of my neck.

"They don't complain," he said with a tense smile as he walked out of the room into the city. I checked my neck in the mirror for bruising. No live person would stand that. He's talking about how to check if someone is dead.

I asked the new professor at Green River Community College about using the jugular vein to take a pulse. She said, "I have concerns about the person who showed you that." I didn't say it was so hard it hurt and almost bruised my neck. I was marked down on the vitals test, even though I followed the correct procedure with the wrist. Medicine wasn't my best field.

August 2001

I'm heading off to graduate school. Moving out of my house and renting it to strangers. Housing is difficult in Pullman. So, I'm putting together items to go into storage. I add my jewelry box and set it on a stack of boxes. A thief needs to go through a keyed gate, then through two locks to find my valuables. The storage owner demands to know if I have anything valuable in the storage locker and where it is. I don't feel comfortable answering his questions, but he is insistent before finalizing the paperwork. I just moved everything into the locker and I didn't want to move it all back out. I admit that I have old coins. The storage owner demands I buy insurance. My father pays the fees for me. I wait at the truck while my father uses the restroom. My father took the lock keys with him and returned them when he came back. My father also said he told Daniel about what I put into storage; defensively he says, "I didn't think anything of it." My father has unwavering trust in Daniel. I don't know if it was the storage facility owner, someone else in the storage office, my father, or Daniel, but my 1927 silver coin was stolen along with all my other coins. The storage owner didn't report the theft to the police and didn't payout on the insurance. He said my father was a suspect.

March 1, 2022

Two state workers sneak past security. I'm standing next to the timeclock on my way out of the building. They talk to me about profiling a murderer. I'll call them Ayako and Ayala.

"What was the name of the first victim?" Ayako questions, "Did he know her a long time?"

"That's not what the book is about," I retort. "I find it offensive that you ask the name of the victim, but don't ask the name of the murderer."

"We are trying to protect the innocent," Ayako defends.

"You have a strange idea of who is innocent. Each and every time you do this you insert the wrong name," I accuse.

"You've only been married once," Ayako asserts. My second husband has had the pleasure of explaining to them that he wasn't my only husband. Translated to my English, this means he is becoming irritated.

"County records don't show up in computer searches as easily as court documents," I explain. "Marriage certificates are county records. Divorce decrees show up because they are actual court documents." Ayala holds up her phone to do a search.

"We're concerned about your safety," Ayako says.

I breathe a sigh of relief, "Finally you're concerned about my safety. This whole time I've been trying to get you to think about my safety." I add, "He says there is only one he let get away. He tried to kill me four times [not including the poisoning attempts] and he's still stalking me."

In a side conversation, I hear, "She meant that as praise," a woman's voice explains to someone next to her. "But they took it as a reprimand because they realized, they haven't been concerned about her safety."

"Let's go," Ayala whispers to Ayako.

A manager says, "You're forgetting it is her book. Who sent the file to you? Did you check?" They look down frowning trying to remember."

"Wait," stops Ayala. "What is that you said about records?"

The manager inserts, "County records are searchable at the county courthouse. You might get lucky finding them in the court documents." The manager adds, "She's not the one delivering a message to the killer. That's you. I know her. You don't. You're terrifying her," the manager reprimands.

Security comes around the corner. "I'm sorry I shouldn't have let you get past," she says, "You need to come with me," leading them away.

Later in the week, I'm at gatekeep. The dayshift AM informs me, "Your water spider keeps getting bombarded with questions." A water spider stocks our boxes. "Do you really think writing this book is worth it?"

"Even the Green River Strangler has friends," I tell him. "My husband was buying shovels from the hardware store one at a time every two weeks."

"Oh I see," he says. "I didn't realize it was about that."

I look around towards the pallets of boxes, "Did you escort the person to security? Usually, it is someone who snuck into the building."

"I always assume it is an associate. I'll be right back," and he leaves to the main greenway.

March 10, 2022

I don't know what transpired. All I know is, after I clocked out to leave at the end of my shift, security was looking straight at me and grinning ear to ear. This is something that never happens.

CONCLUSION

In the Book of Genesis Chapter 15, it was God who walked through the parts. Gary and Daniel misread the symbolism in the passage. This wasn't to show Abraham what would happen to him if he broke the pact. Abraham never walked through. There was never a reason to use human corpses for the pact. The task was for God to show what would happen to Him if He didn't keep up His end of the pact. Gary and Daniel missed the point. It was to show Abraham how much God loved him and how much He would keep His promises. His light comes into the darkness.

1983

When we were on the bridge over where Amina Agisheff was murdered, I insisted on getting out of the old white Toyota sedan, while it was still moving. It had nothing to do with the driver who picked me up as a hitch-hiker. I ran straight to Amina's friend and neighbor, Arnold, who heard the struggle. Arnold was one of the neighbors who called the police when it happened. Arnold knew this was the Green River Killer's first victim. The struggle was slow, loud, and clumsy. It wasn't planned or prepared. He knew it was the first kill. It wasn't in a secluded area. There were two large apartment complexes less than a block away. Amina wasn't a prostitute and she was older than the other victims. Gary didn't have a motive to kill her. And Gary was already a convicted killer, well past being slow, clumsy, and unprepared. Daniel was giving a ride home for his mother's friend each day she completed her work shift as a waitress. His mother praised him for doing a nice thing, but he sometimes resented it.

I wish the pastor hadn't told the group that Daniel seems fine with me. It gave me a burden that no one should need to carry. I wish the pastor's wife hadn't encouraged Daniel to give me a ride home. I honestly felt safer walking the two blocks. But the pastor and his wife paired me together with Daniel and didn't want to take that away from him.

The seafoam green was an unsuccessful attempt to calm Daniel. I never noticed the seafoam green until I described the house while writing this book. I thought the matching interior of the car was just to have a constant color scheme, not to buy a car with seafoam green interior. I didn't realize either Daniel's expectation for seafoam green upholstery or seafoam green paint for the book shelf. I thought he didn't like the mustard yellow sofa, not that he wanted it green. Viola said the seafoam green was for the guests and I took her comment literally. Even when Daniel added half-n-half to crème de menthe and commented on the color and even when the drugs he took were light green, I didn't pick up on it. Not even when Viola gave Daniel the swivel rocker and said, "It is the only color he responds to."

1991

Investigator Ms. Read called my friend Jerry on the phone. I expected Jerry would assure Ms. Read that I had no interest in whomever she was pairing me with. Jerry came by the apartment to counsel me based on what Ms. Read had said to him.

Jerry explains Ms. Read's point of view as I'm sitting outside. The sky is starting to get dark. I can't process it. The words hit my head with a thud, but they won't reassemble into a sentence. All I can do is sit on the grass in front of my apartment and scream uncontrollably at the top of my lungs. Jerry scolds me, "If you don't stop screaming, no one is ever going to listen to you."

No one was listening to me before I started screaming. Finally, I manage to get a sentence out and chant it over and over, "I don't want to be with that man. I don't want to be with that man." I rock back and forth as I'm screaming and taking deep breaths on the front lawn. After Jerry left, the neighbor in my apartment building came out to calm me down. He repeated back what I was screaming. Yes, words were coming out of my mouth and someone could hear them. For a while, I wasn't sure. Someone can understand them. I breathe now with an occasional gasp. I'm calm or at least appear calm, really closer to stoic.

Ms. Read thought Viola Bondehagen was my mother. Viola played along. Dan played the part of my brother, instead of my ex-husband, something he had done many times. Ms. Read assumed they were more credible and that I was mentally ill. Part of my brain knew Ms. Read paired me together with a murderer. I couldn't process who. At first, I thought it was Mr. Clark, who was a fraud and also a murderer. Now I realize it was with my ex-husband who Ms. Read assumed to be a more credible brother, to explain the same last name.

Ms. Read didn't want to take the time to read my complaint. She didn't want to take a statement from me directly because she assumed that step was completed. So she contacted others instead to fill her in. But she contacted people I hadn't shared my complaint with. When she did so, she picked up a case that was eight years prior. This follows me year after year and again this month.

The CWU attorney, Ms. Kulik, submits to Halverson & Applegate a request that I do not speak with a list of about 200 people. None of these people on the list had ever requested 'no contact'. There is no rationale for the 'no contact'. I'm not to have contact with the state attorneys. I'm only allowed to contact them through my attorney. But I'm not allowed to have contact with my own attorney either. I'm supposed to use the attorney they designate as my power of attorney. (There was no competency hearing to justify this.) And they designate my mother as my power of attorney. But I'm also not allowed to have contact with either my mother or my father. My parents are both listed as well for 'no contact'. I'm not allowed to contact the police. I'm not allowed to contact the sheriff. I'm not allowed to contact anyone at CWU including both current and former professors and students. This has baffled me for 30 years. March 11, 2022, I'm finally getting this. The CWU attorney, like Ms. Nightingale and Ms. Read, thought Viola Bondehagen was my mother. The CWU attorney was requesting for me to only have contact with Viola, the woman who tried to sell me to human trafficking. The attorney regarded her as my power of attorney. This is why they thought I'd agree to be a prostitute.

1994

Daniel was mortified about lethal injection because serial killer John Wayne Gacy, who played "Patches the Clown", was executed that year. Daniel would see Patches each time he saw a picture or statue of a clown. From Daniel's perspective, it was Patches who was the serial killer, not Gacy. Daniel responded as if Patches was giving him instructions. Thomas and Viola intended to teach their son about stranger danger. But he became permanently unhinged. His tense smile and laugh was his imitation of the clown persona.

1991

Fortunately there was someone who heard my response, Abby. Abby was the one who encouraged me to tell my story and bring light into the darkness. She owned the house next door to my apartment. She must have heard my conversation with Jerry and heard me screaming on the lawn. Not only that, Abby was the owner of the Subway Restaurant. She was the woman behind the sandwich counter quietly waiting while I talked with the Halverson & Applegate attorney about my case, the same attorney who argued against an evaluation for incompetency. The attorney whose statement was stricken from the record as too biased. The attorney whose bar card was suspended by Ms. Kulik for refusing to go along with the attempt to commit. Abby never moved while we talked. She just looked at us and quietly smiled. Abby must have understood the case more than anyone.

2015

The Student Conduct Board at the graduate college used the FBI flagged file that describes Viola instead of me. The FBI also expunged my case because the order was incomplete and never filed or served. Everyone involved in the attempt to commit was indicted across the board. That is the file WSU used to have me expelled. WSU submitted a statement, "Sometime during March 2015, the Respondent approached the Director of Human Resources at WSU – Vancouver, without the Complainant's knowledge, to discuss whether she was permitted to invite the Complainant to social activities and/or pursue a romantic relationship with the Complainant". That wasn't my reason for the meeting with HR. My side of the story is completely missing from the file. The instructor asked me to come to his apartment to eat take and bake pizza and watch a Redbox movie. There would be no one with me except him. I didn't feel comfortable being alone with him. With my history, I deserve to be cautious. This was my reason for the meeting with HR, not to discuss pursuing a relationship. I was finishing up my Master's degree and had already defended my thesis. This is completely missing too. The underlying impression to the board was that I was working on my Bachelor's degree and pursuing a current professor. There are so many things wrong with that portrayal. It's hard to even know where to begin to address it.

My statements were taken out of context. When my actual testimony did not fit with the new context, my testimony was deleted. I'm answering the question, "Why did the FBI flag the file?" This is the question the WSU Student Conduct

Board asked, even though the question was just a ploy to discuss an expunged criminal case. I'm putting things together for the first time. I'm finding more reasons than the FBI knew. This is my witness statement. I will sign and notarize each and every page, and copyright so no one can change my testimony.

BOTTLE OF PURE NARD

I'm shifting focus. Mary of Bethany and Mary the Magdalene wanted to serve Jesus. Mary anointed Jesus's feet. The Pharisee accused Mary of being a prostitute and the label stuck. According to a neighbor and friend, Amina was

a nice woman. Amina was working as a waitress serving customers, and was mislabeled as a prostitute. I wanted to serve Jesus. Instead, I was mislabeled as a prostitute. Mary the Magdalene, Amina, and I have something in common. So, I wrote a song called Bottle of Pure Nard (Jesus's Feet).

Key of C
Jesus told Martha not to fret. I stayed at his feet, heard the rest.
Today I sit at Jesus' feet and feel his love for me.
I threw myself at Jesus' feet. "Lord if you had been here," I mourned in defeat,
He raised Lazarus from the dead. The news of the miracle spread.
Tears of joy and sadness bottled up inside my heart,
poured out on Jesus' feet with the bottle of pure nard.
My tears and sobs would not retreat. I had no towel to cool his feet.
In the Pharisees' house I prayed, uncovered my hair; took down my braid.
My hair absorbed the dirt and heat. I kissed his feet. I was

indiscreet.

There was no one left to condemn, near this man from Bethlehem.

Tears of joy and sadness bottled up inside my heart

as hard as stone, poured out on Jesus' feet with the bottle of pure nard.

We had anointing oils and nard. How would we get past the

guard?

I clung to the feet of my Lord. Jesus' life has been restored.

Tears of joy and sadness bottled up inside my heart,

poured out on Jesus' feet with the bottle of pure nard,

with the bottle of pure nard. My brokenness is gone.

DOWN TO THE WATER

It was in early August 1983. I finished my summer session classes for the day. Instead of waiting for the bus, I left to enjoy the outdoors while taking a shortcut. "Don't cut through the woods," a Green River Community College classmate warned. "There is a man in there who is really demented. The police have been trying to catch him." Another warned, "Don't go through there!" And another shouted, "There are bodies wrapped in plastic."

I imagined a deranged homeless man splattered with drops of blood. I shook my head. "It's okay. My boyfriend said, 'It should be alright,'" I replied. I ducked into the forest to take the shortcut.

"Wait!" the classmate yelled. His upper mouth was raised to show his top teeth as he thought. His eyes looked up towards the sky, as his eyebrows lowered. "The only person who would tell you it was safe to go through the woods would be the killer." He turned to a friend, "Why would her boyfriend say it is safe unless he's the one who committed the murders?"

"I don't know," the friend said. "Just leave her." He led the classmate back towards campus. "Some women are just stupid."

I walked home through the trees. The forest was peaceful and vacant. The path through the trees was clear, wide, and easy to follow. But there was no food to forage. There was less vegetation than I expected. And no people. No deranged homeless man. No bodies wrapped in plastic. There were last year's leaves lying on the ground, green sword ferns, and some scattered bushes. I walked out to the main road and hiked down the hill.

I made a comment about the lack of vegetation in the woods to a man in the student building at the college. The man gravely responded, "There's a reason for that." He didn't explain

At the apartment complex, Amina's neighbor explained, "I called the police. Six or eight neighbors called. Look at the area. It's not isolated." He waved his hands at the three apartment complexes in the area. "The police didn't get here fast enough," Amina's neighbor angrily complained. "They couldn't find the couple arguing." His voice was softer now, "They went down to the water and looked. They waited for thirty minutes." He had a look of resolution. His eyebrows furrowed as he said, "I think he was still down there."

[This was in 1982. There was no 911 service or cell phones. At that time callers dialed zero for the operator from a land phone. The operator patched the call through to the police station. If there are several calls from one location, the operator scrubbed the calls down to the caller with the most information. This neighbor was the one the operator selected for the police to gain information from.]

"The police didn't believe me, "Amina's neighbor complained. His voice was deep. He felt grieved to the bone. Remembering the event made him unsteady and troubled. Now he seemed less certain, "I told the police which car I thought was his. But they wouldn't have it. It was a light green one." He gestured across towards the parking lot. "The police looked up the license plate number," he looked forward. The summer sun reflected off his eyes. "The police said they talked to the owner, and he was an old man who never left home." Amina's neighbor shook his head and added, "The police wondered why he'd park there when she was almost home to her kids. The police insisted on waiting 48 hours to report her as a missing person."

The police didn't mention the car in the police report. I was sure they would. Thomas was an old man. He had a light green car. I went to talk to him. It was the first thing I did. But Thomas told me some topics weren't discussed. I thought I made an error in social etiquette. I didn't realize the subject was just taboo in their house.

After I moved to the studio apartment in Kent, I was tired of providing financially for Daniel and hoped he would get a job. This had gone on for months. He mentioned that he was certified as a lifeguard. I looked in the newspaper classified ads for lifeguard openings.

He shook his head, "I can't," he said. "They'd drown. They won't let you work as a lifeguard if you've had someone drown." He explained, "In universal lifeguard training, we learned to stop the person from struggling in the water. Sometimes you have to knock the person out, so they don't pull you down in the water," Daniel explained. "You have to hit them on the top of the head like this." He demonstrated restraining a person with his left arm and hitting them on the top of the head with his right fist and middle knuckle. "When they are unconscious, they float."

It seemed hopeless. I stopped looking for lifeguard jobs for him. I talked to a staffing specialist. "It isn't true," the staffing specialist said. "They don't keep you from working as a lifeguard if someone drowned." She pondered for a moment and looked at me intently. "It must be something else," she decided and walked away.

In late April 1984, Daniel said, "My parents invited us to go to Auburn today."

I knew visits with his family were important to him. "Can we go to our church in Seattle first?" I asked. He agreed. So, we went to the United Methodist Church in Seattle. After church, we drove to Auburn to visit Daniel's parents. Viola prepared Daniel's favorite meal, turkey rice casserole. She made it with just four ingredients: turkey, rice, condensed cream of celery soup, and water. After the dinner prayer, Daniel sat at the table, looked down at his plate, and wiggled his fingers in anticipation. This made Viola smile. After dinner we cleaned up.

Viola stood in the dining room and suggested, "You could earn a Montessori certificate. It takes less time than a degree." Daniel started to approach from the living room with a look of intent. Viola looked startled and frightened. "Some words are off limits," Viola said to the family. Her voice was low and quiet. "Apparently, Montessori is one of them."

"Along with certain names," Thomas firmly interjected. He stood up from the sofa and stepped toward the dining room.

Viola had a contemplative look and took a sideways glance at Daniel. "We waited for you to come home," Viola told Daniel. "We weren't sure if we should wait or start eating dinner." She paused, "We waited for about an hour or so. When it was past seven, we ate dinner."

"It was past eight," Thomas grumbled. He stood in the living room, hunched over. He stared at Daniel with a scrutinizing look of judgment.

Viola shrugged at Thomas. She looked at Daniel in concern. She continued to talk, "When you finally came home, it was dark, and you were sopping wet." She looked at Daniel from head to toe and back up again.

"And my shovel was missing," Thomas added in irritation.

Daniel turned to face Thomas. "I brought it back," Daniel said defensively.

"That's not the point," Thomas replied. "The police came and asked me about the car. You know I never bought insurance for you. I told them your mother drove her home."

Viola nodded with certainty, "I'm happy to do it."

Daniel looked at his mother and briefly smiled.

Viola explained to Daniel, "She told me in church how her feet hurt so badly at the end of her shift. I couldn't let her walk home."

"I just wanted it to stop," Daniel complained.

"We asked you to drive her as a household chore," Viola explained. This meant the task was in exchange for staying at the house, receiving food, and not paying rent. Daniel looked at his mother and soaked this in.

"I figured you ran a red light with the car," Thomas explained to Daniel. "I need to know what I lied to."

Daniel looked back at his father. Daniel gave Thomas his full attention, but there were no words in response. His mouth remained closed.

"Does this have something to do with the person who drowned?" I asked Viola. They looked confused. I turned towards Daniel, "You said you couldn't be a lifeguard anymore because you had someone drown."

"Well, that answers that question," Viola responded.

Daniel admitted, "I knew I could overpower her in the water." He looked over at his father. It was a look of accusation.

"Which one of you decided to move there?" Thomas asked. Daniel pointed to me and smiled.

"I decided to move there," I said with assertion.

[I didn't know Amina's body was recently found next to my studio apartment. Thomas and Viola didn't know Daniel dug her up, moved her body, and reburied her.]

Viola had a look of anger. I assumed her anger was directed at me. I didn't understand the conversation. I answered Viola's question, but she didn't answer mine.

It took me 40 years to fill in the blanks: "That's not the point," Thomas replied [to Daniel]. "The police came and asked me about [my] car. You know I never bought [auto] insurance for you. [I didn't tell the police you were driving my car without auto insurance.] I told them your mother drove [Amina] home [in my car from the restaurant]." No one was allowed to use Amina's name. Her name was off-limits. I didn't breach social etiquette when I asked Thomas about her. They didn't talk about it for a different reason. I didn't put it together until after the first edition was published.

"No one doubts your story," the police officer said. "Your apartment was one of the ones close to Meeker Street Bridge," he said. He expected me to know. He didn't realize he was informing me of new information.

I avoided watching the news. I never looked on a map to see where Meeker Street Bridge was. I assumed it was in Auburn down from Main Street on the way to Green River Community College. But, no, the map showed it was in Kent. I walked over that bridge twice a day, sometimes four times a day. At the time it was going on, my apartment wasn't just one of the apartments near Meeker Street Bridge, it was the apartment closest to Meeker Street Bridge. And this was the location of Amina's body when it was found.

After police found bodies near Meeker Street Bridge, my neighbor met me on the front porch and told me, "Ask [Daniel] what is at that group of trees across the road."

One day as Daniel drove home, I got up the courage to ask, "What is that over there?" I pointed to the left as he drove the car south.

"Why?" Daniel asked.

"It looks pretty. Is there a park? Maybe we can visit." I tried to sound pleasant.

"No park," Daniel said. He turned sharply to look at me with a scowl. It was a brief gesture. "You're the one who wanted to live here." I wanted to move to Kent. Daniel wanted to stay in Seattle. "If it were up to me, I'd be as far away from it as possible," Daniel informed me.

I frowned. I had a questioning expression. I didn't understand why he wanted to be far away from here. He didn't need to move in with me. He could live on his own. "What is wrong with the river?" I asked.

"You don't understand. I spent hours in that water. It was cold. Although that helped," Daniel said.

"Didn't you go downstream?" I asked. "If I were in the water for hours, I would be washed away with the current."

"I'm strong," Daniel answered. He had tread water. He looked down at the baseboard and had a miserable expression. "The Green River isn't green, it's black. I've never seen anything so black." He turned his face towards me and asked, "How long can you hold your breath underwater?"

"Not long," I replied. I can hold my breath for 40 seconds. The average person can hold their breath for 30 to 90 seconds. The world record is 24 minutes, 3 seconds.

Daniel didn't wait for my answer. "Guess how long I can hold my breath underwater," he said.

"Maybe 13 minutes," I guessed.

"Reverse those numbers. I can hold my breath underwater for 31 minutes," Daniel said. "That day it was closer to 34 minutes. I had to wait until they left."

After we got home, I told the neighbor, "He didn't want to talk about it."

The neighbor answered, "That bad, huh," the neighbor retreated inside his apartment. He didn't explain.

Later, I asked my pastor, "Do you know what that river is?"

My pastor said, "It's the Green River." He was surprised I didn't know. I was impressed that the river ran through both Auburn and Kent. At the time I didn't think of anything more than that.

All the information hit me like a bag of bricks as I put this together. When Daniel buried his first kill, she was seven miles from his parents' house. Then he dug up Amina's body and reburied her. He didn't move her further away. He moved her body closer, and right next to my apartment. Amina was found shortly after she was reburied. If I hadn't argued with Daniel, Amina would be in the original burial spot and her body not found.

When Daniel asked me to move to a one-bedroom apartment, I didn't know Amina's body was found buried next to my studio apartment. Daniel told me to put the one-bedroom apartment in my name, only my name. I realize now he didn't want to be traced. He said we could afford it. I expected Daniel to help pay the rent on the one-bedroom. Instead, I was stuck with the monthly bills. He asked my parents for additional money. Between Daniel burying the new shovel in the dumpster under sacks of garbage and Amina's body found buried in the field next to my studio apartment, it wouldn't have taken long for people to figure it out.

When Thomas and Viola drove up from California to visit, they expected to stay with friends from the church. Instead, they visited us at the one-bedroom apartment and stayed there, Viola asked, "Why did you move to this apartment? Is it to be further away from the Green River Killer?"

Daniel and I both started talking at the same. Daniel began to say, "If we weren't in a one-bedroom, you wouldn't be able to visit."

I started to say, "I suppose it is further away." I was doubtful the distance was much of a difference. I was told the area was Midway, a part of Des Moines.

Thomas stopped Daniel. Thomas held out his arm and said, "Wait, I want to know what she thinks."

"The police say the suspect is another police officer in the Midway area."

"In Midway!" Viola said and smiled with a nod.

"That is how he knew who worked as prostitutes. He had access to view police arrest records," I explained and paused. "But he doesn't fit. I don't think it as a police officer. I think it was an overzealous religious person. Maybe someone from the Assembly of God Church."

"A holy roller!" Viola exclaimed. I nodded. "She thinks it was a holy roller," Viola confirmed. She looked at Daniel and smiled.

"I wonder what I said to make her think that," Daniel pondered.

Daniel talked about the black color of the Green River. It doesn't look black when you stand next to it. The water looks black when shaded from the sun. The overpass put the Green River in a shadow. He was under the overpass treading water. He had Amina's body secured between his legs. The limp body held between his legs helped keep him afloat. He had to keep track of the body and not let it float away until he decided where to bury it.

Arugula becomes angry with me, feeling that I am letting Gary Ridgway off the hook for Amina's murder. My response: Ridgway was never charged with Amina's murder. He didn't know Amina. There was nothing to connect him to her murder, except for the burial location. Amina doesn't fit the profile of his other kills. There was no DNA evidence to link him to Amina's murder. There was DNA evidence to link Ridgway to the other 49 murders. He confessed to all of those. Ridgway venomously denied killing Amina. Why confess to the other murders and deny this one? Ridgway is doing 49 consecutive life sentences of solitary confinement. A change in the number of life sentences wouldn't impact his confinement.

Consider that meanwhile, the person who committed Amina's murder was left at large. The social worker's anonymous file says to "wait until she starts to walk away, and then stop her." In the first chapter of this book, a woman stood outside my church and called,

"Mary," as I started to walk away. She looked like she was hailing a taxi. She misunderstood my name. But she followed the instructions in the file by preventing me from walking away.

This action repeats what Daniel did to Amina. Daniel waited until Amina was almost home to her two children. She switched her role from waitress to mother. Amina imagined their expectant faces. She started to walk away, and he stopped her. Before Amina had an opportunity to open her front door, Daniel stopped her. He dragged her across the street and under the overpass.

Each time the social workers stop me, they recreate what the first victim went through. Instead of turning from his stress trigger, Daniel pressed into the trigger. He relived the moment as if obsession would relieve his fear. And he encouraged others to perform the same, stopping me as I tried to walk away.

EPILOGUE

Axel came back by my work. "Is it a religious book?" he asked.

"More like sacrilegious," I regretfully answered. "Well, it is sacrilegious when it comes to Genesis 15."

"Is that something to ask Ridgway about?" Axel asked.

"Yes, that would definitely be an interesting conversation," I answered.

"What's on the table?" Axel asked.

"The death of Amina," I answered. "Daniel was giving her rides home from work as a favor to his mother."

"Why didn't his mother report it?" Axel asked.

"Two reasons," I explained. "She didn't want him going through the system and she was frightened. I didn't hear the conversation. I was busy doing dishes in the kitchen. For a brief moment I saw a frightened look on her face."

"What was the conversation before?" Axel asked.

"She was praising him for giving her friend a ride home as a nice thing to do. He didn't want her to bring it up," I recalled. "There was tension in the room and I couldn't break through it."

"That would explain why she was older than the other victims," Axel commented.

"And one more thing, if you show a picture of a clown to my ex- husband. You'll need to be careful."

"So ask Gary Ridgway about Genesis 15 and if your ex-husband sees a picture of a clown, wear padded body armor," he clarified.

"Yes," I said, wincing as I watched him walk back up the stairs towards the exit, "Be safe."

At the Walla Walla State Prison, "What's on the table?" Ridgway asks. "The death of Amina," Axel answered.

I confessed to everything else," Ridgway said, "If I killed her, why would I deny it. It doesn't make sense."

"I'll put in a nice word to the judge," Axel encouraged.

"I know the passage," Ridgway said, pushing the Bible on the table. Ridgway asked, "Do you have him?"

"Do we have who?" Axel asked. "Does the passage remind you of someone?"

"Oh, come on," Ridgeway said. "You didn't come here to hear me read." Ridgway asked again, "Do you have him?"

"What is his name?" Axel asked. "You're safe in here. He won't get far," Axel assured.

"I don't remember his name," Ridgway answered. "He was a Norwegian guy, tall with blond hair." Ridgway is shown a recent picture. "It's hard to tell." Then a younger picture, "Yes, that's him," Ridgway confirmed. "We were both going bald in the same way." Ridgway clarified, "I already had the bodies. He said he had his own. The stupid #@&% wanted to cut them in two. I convinced him not to. I don't remember how. I didn't want them desecrated."

In California, "Another one with an aversion to clowns."

"All I could find was a picture of a clown." Watching from the one- way glass window, "This is unexpected."

A woman opens the door to the viewing room and loudly asks, "Is it time to—"

"Shush," he says firmly.

She is quickly silent. She walks in and stands near to watch through the one-way glass. She asks, "Does he think the clown is his legal counsel?"

April 20, 2022

The man who entered the building to talk with the water spider came back. He was charged with trespassing. Later he sent one of his employees to ask questions from the list. His employee said he is a senior state worker. They think my ex-husband's name is Mike. They think that I believe I'm the mother of the messiah. I can't shake them out of it. My supervisor says I'll need to write another book. It will be titled, *Hephzibah and the Dragon.*

www.ingramcontent.com/pod-product-compliance
Lightning Source LLC
Chambersburg PA
CBHW052206270326
41931CB00011B/2241